Library of
Davidson College

VOID

Occasional Paper Series 5

Political and Military Implications of the "Nuclear Winter" Theory

by Allen Lynch

Institute for East-West Security Studies

*The Occasional Paper Series
of the Institute for East-West Security Studies*
features articles on critical issues of international security and East-West relations by a broad range of policy specialists, officials and academics from East and West. The purpose of the series is to foster serious analysis and discussion between East and West on issues which affect international security. Articles published in this series represent solely the views of the authors, and not necessarily those of the Institute, its Board of Directors, or its staff.

Occasional Paper Series 5

Political and Military Implications of the "Nuclear Winter" Theory

by Allen Lynch

Institute for East-West Security Studies

WESTVIEW PRESS * BOULDER, COLORADO

The Carnegie Corporation of New York
generously provided support for
this study, its publication and dissemination

Allen Lynch is a Research Associate
at the Institute for East-West Security Studies

Distributed by
Westview Press, Inc.
5500 Central Avenue
Boulder, Colorado 80301

Cover Design: Hersch Wartik, Inc.
Copyright © 1987, Institute for East-West Security Studies, Inc.
ISBN 0-913449-03-2

ISBN 0-8133-0658-2 (Westview)

The Institute for East-West Security Studies is the only permanent center to bring East and West together to engage in sustained dialogue, study and research on security issues which affect countries of both the NATO and Warsaw Treaty Organization alliances.

Established in 1981 as an independent international initiative, the Institute brings to New York for a ten-month period each year up to a dozen scholars and officials from a broad range of countries in Europe and North America to examine political, economic, and military problems of East-West security. Their work is supplemented by study groups, conferences, seminars, lectures, and publications, as well as by regular meetings of a Board of Directors and an Academic Advisory Committee composed of prominent persons from East and West. The Institute publishes an *East-West Monograph Series,* an *Occasional Paper Series, East-West Notes* and *Conference Reports* on a regular basis.

The Institute's work is directed toward identifying policy-oriented options to enhance stability, reduce antagonisms and the dangers of conflict, and expand East-West cooperation. The Institute's sustained East-West interaction process is designed to help clarify differences in perception, search for ways of building on shared concerns, and stimulate new ideas for improving security for both East and West.

The Institute values its independence and accepts no government monies. As a not-for-profit organization, tax-exempt in the U.S., it is completely financed by foundations, corporations and individuals in Europe and the U.S. European governments are encouraged to and do provide in-kind contributions including the hosting of major conferences and meetings.

FOREWORD

For more than forty years, the primary utility ascribed to nuclear weapons has been as a deterrent against the use of military force. Nonetheless, nuclear powers have developed plans for the use of these weapons in the event of extreme situations—the strategy of possible first-use of nuclear weapons, for example, remains part of NATO policy. The nuclear winter theory holds that the soot and smoke from burning cities and forests following a large nuclear strike would result in a potentially catastrophic cooling of the earth's climate. By highlighting the suicidal consequences of even a "successful" use of nuclear weapons, the nuclear winter theory challenges the credibility of deterrence policies and calls into question the validity of the U.S. nuclear guarantee to Western Europe. This theory raises some of the most fundamental questions about the military policies of both alliances.

This study is a carefully balanced examination of the implications of the nuclear winter theory. The author, Dr. Allen Lynch, a Research Associate at the Institute for East-West Security Studies in New York, has undertaken research and discussion on this matter in the United States and the Soviet Union, and he examines the positions of proponents, skeptics, and opponents of the theory. His analysis of the significance of the nuclear winter theory is one of the most readable and thorough accounts available, and provides many useful insights into the approaches of Washington and Moscow to this issue.

The main contributions of this paper are Dr. Lynch's suggestions concerning the political and military implications of the nuclear winter theory. Since the theory was first described in a Western journal in 1983, significant and complex research has been undertaken in the U.S., Europe, and the Soviet Union—none of which has refuted the theory, which appears to present a plausible picture of the outcome of nuclear war. The Pentagon's major study on this idea accepted the nuclear winter theory, and yet concluded that it had no practical impact on U.S. policies and doctrines. Dr. Lynch raises some fundamental questions about the military and political implications of this matter, phrasing his concerns in terms of policy choices for East and West, and thus providing a valuable contribution to the current debate about strategic stability and nuclear doctrine which opened up as a result of the Reagan-Gorbachev meetings of the past year.

Allen Lynch received his Ph.D. from Columbia University, where he studied at the W. Averell Harriman Institute for the Advanced Study of the Soviet Union. He is the author of *The Soviet Study of International Relations* (forthcoming) from Cambridge University Press. A specialist on the Soviet Union and U.S.-USSR relations, Dr. Lynch has contributed articles to professional journals and newspapers, and has spoken on national television and radio programs dealing with East-West issues.

The author wishes to pay particular appreciation to the Resident Fellows of the Institute for East-West Security Studies for 1985–86 and 1986–87, to Institute staff members Dr. F. Stephen Larrabee, Kerry S. McNamara and Peter B. Kaufman for their careful and critical reading of the manuscript in various drafts, and to Dr. Thomas Malone, Scholar in Residence at St. Joseph's College, for his technical advice. The Institute gratefully acknowledges the support of the Carnegie Corporation of New York for providing support for this study, its publication and dissemination. The views in this paper are solely those of its author and should not be ascribed to the funders or the Institute. The Institute for East-West Security Studies is pleased to sponsor publication of this study as a contribution to the debate in both the East and the West about the most fundamental question of international security.

John Edwin Mroz
President
January 1987

TABLE OF CONTENTS

Foreword	iv
1. The Significance of the Theory of Nuclear Winter	1
Introduction	1
Evolution of the Nuclear Winter Theory	4
Impact on Deterrence	9
2. Nuclear Winter and the Soviet Union	17
3. Political and Military Implications	27
Impact on Strategic Weapons Policies	27
Intra-alliance Relations: NATO and the Warsaw Pact	31
4. The Necessity for Political Leadership	37
Bibliography	47

1

The Significance of the Theory of Nuclear Winter

■ Introduction

Since 1983 a new term has entered the vocabulary of diplomats, military planners, defense policy analysts and ordinary citizens—"nuclear winter." The theory of "nuclear winter," first developed by European and American scientists and since confirmed by colleagues in the academy and government—including the U.S. National Academy of Sciences and the Defense Department—forecasts a previously overlooked consequence of nuclear war. The theory predicts that the soot and smoke from burning cities and forests following large-scale nuclear strikes will seriously reduce the amount of sunlight reaching the earth for weeks and months, causing a cooling of the climate and potentially catastrophic damage to such delicate social-ecological systems as agriculture on a global scale.

More generally, by focusing attention on a combination of immediate and longer-term consequences of nuclear war—physical, atmospheric, ecological, agricultural, and social—the nuclear winter theory suggests that the delayed effects of nuclear war may be at least as destructive as the better-known direct effects of blast, heat, radiation and fallout. The public controversy surrounding the theory since its appearance in 1983 has at times obscured the actual significance, both scientific and political-military, of the research on nuclear winter. Indeed, the policy implications of the nuclear winter effect, which had escaped notice for nearly four decades, have scarcely been explored in any systematic fashion. What follows represents an attempt to map out some of those implications for governments and military in East and West.

Long before the appearance of the nuclear winter theory, most analysts who thought seriously about the problems posed by nuclear weapons realized that there were probably unforeseeable side effects to the use of these weapons and that these side effects might prove as deadly as the direct blast and heat effects of nuclear explosions. The inventors of the atomic bomb, for example, worried that an atomic explosion might burn up the atmosphere.[1] In the aftermath of Hiroshima and Nagasaki, atomic radiation was identified as an additional lethal consequence of the nuclear explosion which, if not immediately fatal, could work its effects on generations yet unborn. In 1954 another unforeseen side effect—radioactive fallout from one of the first hydrogen bomb tests—contaminated Japanese fishermen and Micronesian islanders in the Pacific. Public concern about this helped lead to the eventual conclusion of the first significant arms control treaty between the United States and the Soviet Union, the Limited Nuclear Test-Ban Treaty of 1963. Later, research sponsored by the U.S. government revealed that a series of nuclear explosions could seriously deplete the ozone layer in the upper atmosphere, thereby exposing the earth to an intolerable degree of ultraviolet radiation from the sun.[2] In the early 1980s physicians from around the world organized to underscore some of the sociological consequences of nuclear war, in particular the complete breakdown of society's medical infrastructure and the corresponding inability to treat the overwhelming majority of those injured by the immediate blast, heat, and radiation effects of atomic explosions.[3]

All of these effects, once unknown or overlooked, are now clearly established facts. These, of course, have to be added to the horrendous primary effects of the nuclear explosion: the blinding light, the irresistible shock wave, and the scorching heat wave setting fires for miles around. Conservative U.S. government estimates of the casualties

---

1. Albert Wohlstetter, "Between an Unfree World and None," *Foreign Affairs*, Summer 1985, p. 964.
2. *Long-Term Worldwide Effects of Multiple Nuclear-Weapons Detonations* (Washington, D.C.: National Academy of Sciences, 1975).
3. Ruth Adams and Susan Cullen (eds.), *The Final Epidemic: Physicians and Scientists on Nuclear War* (Chicago: Educational Foundation for Nuclear Science, 1981); and Yevgeny I. Chazov, L.A. Il'in and A.K. Gus'kova, *Yadernaya voyna: mediko-biologicheskiye posledstviya. Tochka zreniya sovetskikh uchenykh-medikov* [Nuclear War: Medical-Biological Consequences. The Viewpoint of Soviet Scientists and Doctors] (Moscow: Novosti, 1984).

from only the immediate effects of a large-scale nuclear war that included cities as targets indicate that 50–90 million deaths (and possibly as many as 155–165 million deaths) and 30 million injuries could occur in the United States alone.[4] Organized urban society would immediately cease to exist. The secondary fires that would grow a few hours after the initial attack would kill those unable to escape the cities. Local fallout would begin to fall almost immediately, eventually contaminating one-quarter or more of the U.S. with lethal levels of radiation, threatening a further 12–18 million people with doses of radiation fatal within one or two months. An additional 40–50 million Americans would experience sufficient contamination over the following weeks to assure their deaths within several months. "The end results of these immediate effects," writes Dr. Mark A. Harwell, scientist at the Ecosystems Research Center of Cornell University, "could be one-half to three-fourths of the U.S. population as eventual fatalities, and another 15–20 percent as injuries." Comparable figures apply to the Soviet Union.[5]

The point needs little elaboration. The public seems well aware of the unimaginable magnitude of the catastrophe inherent in the use of nuclear weapons. Eighty-nine percent of those Americans polled in 1984 agreed that "there can be no winner in an all-out nuclear war; (that) both the U.S. and the Soviet Union would be completely destroyed." Eighty-three percent agreed that "we cannot be certain that life on earth will continue after a nuclear war." Even more striking, 76 percent disagreed with the assertion that "the idea that all life on earth could be destroyed in a nuclear war is a 'wild exaggeration'."[6]

With so many different ways of dying, in both the short and long run, it would appear superfluous to identify still further ways of doing in human civilization. This applies to the military as well as to the civilian population, for, given the superiority of offense over defense

---

4. Office of Technology Assessment, *The Effects of Nuclear War* (Washington, D.C.: U.S. Government Printing Office, 1979), pp. 94–95, 100.

5. Mark A. Harwell, *Nuclear Winter. The Human and Environmental Consequences of Nuclear War* (New York: Springer-Verlag, 1984), pp. 154–155, 161. See also Frank Barnaby and Joseph Rotblat, "The Effects of Nuclear Weapons," *Ambio*, vol. 11, no. 2–3, 1982, pp. 84–93.

6. *Voter Options on Nuclear Arms Policy* (New York: The Public Agenda Foundation, 1984), p. 24.

inherent in nuclear weapons[7] and the redundant weapons systems fielded by the U.S. and USSR, no military force can ever hope to defend its country against nuclear attack. National survival for the U.S. and USSR is thus essentially dependent upon the decision of the other. If leaders in either country were to decide to destroy the other (or at least, in the jargon of strategic planners, to inflict "unacceptable damage"), the execution of such a decision would be purely a technical, and not a military consideration. There are no military options either nation could devise to prevent such destruction. Nuclear "deterrent" forces affect each superpower's *will* to annihilate the other, not their capacity to do so. This condition of "mutual superiority"—reflecting the utter vulnerability of each country's society and the relative invulnerability of their retaliatory forces—has prevailed certainly since the late 1960s, when the USSR achieved numerical nuclear parity with the U.S., and probably as soon as the USSR was able to strike even a few American cities in a retaliatory strike (in the late 1950s–early '60s). In short, the nuclear age has made the traditional function of the military—"defending" the nation—obsolete. Bernard Brodie, the doyen of American strategic thinkers, recognized this in a remarkable book published in 1946 in which he argued that, whereas heretofore the purpose of the military had been to fight wars, now it must be to prevent them.[8]

■ Evolution of the Nuclear Winter Theory

Given all this, the attention that has been devoted since 1982 to the "nuclear winter" theory at first seems rather remarkable. The "nuclear winter" hypothesis was first raised in its current

---

7. The superiority of the nuclear offense over defense consists simply in the incredible destructiveness of each warhead. In the pre-nuclear era, an attrition rate of 10 percent was considered a major defeat for a bomber force: at that rate, one's ability to prosecute an air war—especially in relation to the marginal damage that any single raid could inflict—would soon be destroyed. In the nuclear era, a population defense would have to be nearly 100 percent effective to avoid the catastrophe an enemy would try to inflict—especially considering the relative cheapness of nuclear weapons and their delivery vehicles (compared to the non-nuclear forces needed to wreak the same effect and to the value of the target—say a city—to be destroyed).

8. Bernard Brodie (ed.), *The Absolute Weapon: Atomic Power and World Order* (Salem, NH: Ayer Co., reprint of 1946 edition), p. 76.

form by Paul J. Crutzen and John W. Birks in an article published in *Ambio*, the journal of the Royal Swedish Academy of Sciences, in 1982. Though the possibility that smoke was released into the atmosphere following a nuclear war had been raised earlier, particularly in a 1966 RAND study[9] and the 1975 report of the U.S. National Academy of Sciences,[10] Crutzen and Birks were the first to perform a systematic analysis of the possible climatic consequences of the smoke that would be released as a result of the massive forest fires ignited by a nuclear war. The operational scenario employed by Crutzen and Birks assumed the detonation of 5,750 megatons of nuclear explosives on a combination of military and urban-industrial targets. The authors also assumed that most weapons employed would have an explosive yield of less than one megaton. This is consistent with the pattern of nuclear weapons development in both the U.S. and USSR, which in recent years has focused on smaller yields on ever more accurate delivery vehicles. It also implies that relatively few nitrogen oxides will be injected into the stratosphere: ozone depletion would not then follow as a direct consequence of a large-scale nuclear war. Yet Crutzen and Birks concluded that other profound effects on the atmosphere could be expected following a large-scale nuclear war.

The authors held that a large-scale nuclear war would cause vast areas of forest to go up in smoke, corresponding at least to the combined land mass of Denmark, Norway and Sweden. In addition, tremendous fires would burn for weeks in cities and industrial areas, and across crop-lands. Furthermore, they held it likely that at least 1.5 billion tons of stored fossil fuels (mostly oil and gas) would be destroyed. These fires would inject a thick smoke layer into the upper atmosphere, drastically reducing the amount of sunlight reaching the earth's surface. The reduction in sunlight would range from 50 percent to 99 percent, depending on circumstances. The ensuing darkness would persist for many weeks, rendering much agricultural activity in the northern hemisphere virtually impossible if the war takes place during the growing season.[11]

---

9. E.S. Batten, *The Effects of Nuclear War on the Weather and Climate* (Santa Monica, CA: The Rand Corporation, Memorandum RM-4989-TAB, August 1966), p. 44, passim.
10. Op. cit.
11. Paul J. Crutzen and John W. Birks, "The Atmosphere after a Nuclear War: Twilight at Noon," *Ambio*, volume 11, no. 2–3, 1982, p. 115.

Following on this initial analysis of Crutzen and Birks, Harwell has noted, "This would begin the series of ecological effects that would persist for years."[12] First, photosynthesis, essential to all plant life, and therefore plant productivity, would be significantly reduced. The drops in temperature that would follow would cause the widespread death of trees and crop plants, animals and unprotected humans. The period of maximum darkness and maximum cold would thus coincide with the onset of mass starvation. Soon thereafter, bodies of freshwater would freeze, in some cases up to a thickness of one meter. The deterioration of sanitary systems combined with the contamination of a limited water supply would lead to the outbreak of infectious diseases on a mass scale. The eventual reemergence of the sun would encourage the spread of insect- and rodent-born diseases, such as the plague. The southern hemisphere, which would be severely affected by the cut-off of food exports from the north, could also experience serious climatic changes. "No place on Earth," Harwell concludes, "could be relied upon to have benign environmental and societal conditions after a large-scale nuclear war.[13]

A number of the assumptions and conclusions reached by theorists of "nuclear winter" have been questioned by skeptics. In the main, these challenge the realism of the scenarios for nuclear war that have been employed, the adequacy of the atmospheric models used, as well as the suggestion that, even in the worst case, the survival of mankind itself might be threatened. Continuing research in this field, though, appears to confirm the validity of Crutzen and Birk's main finding: that a finite number of nuclear explosions will have a global climatic impact.[14] While recent scientific work has served to qualify

---

12. Harwell, op. cit., p. 161.
13. Ibid., pp. 161–164. A major interdisciplinary, international research effort confirmed and detailed these conclusions. See the two-volume study published on behalf of the Scientific Committee on Problems of the Environment (SCOPE) of the International Council of Scientific Unions: *Environmental Consequences of Nuclear War*. Volume I. Physical and Atmospheric Effects, by A. Barrie Pittock, Thomas P. Ackerman, Paul J. Crutzen, Michael C. MacCracken, Charles S. Shapiro, and Richard P. Turco (Chichester: John Wiley & Sons, 1986); Volume II. Ecological and Agricultural Effects, by Mark A. Harwell and Thomas C. Hutchinson (Chichester: John Wiley & Sons, 1985).
14. For earlier work, see R.P. Turco et al., "Nuclear Winter: Global Consequences of Multiple Nuclear Explosions," *Science*, volume 222, no. 4630, December 23, 1983, pp 1283–1292; Anne Ehrlich, "Nuclear Winter," *Bulletin of the Atomic Scientists*, April 1984, pp. 3C–14C. For more recent work, see the two SCOPE

the apocalyptic implications attributed to earlier versions of the theory, the principle of a nuclear winter effect has been confirmed time and again. Starley L. Thompson and Stephen H. Schneider of the National Center for Atmospheric Research in Boulder, Colorado, whose work has been invoked by some as a refutation of the main lines of the theory, in fact confirmed the findings of the National Academy of Sciences and SCOPE that, though the precise magnitude of the effect is difficult to gauge, very large climatic effects are possible and should not be ignored.[15] Taking into account (as the previously cited SCOPE study does) the synergistic effect of a variety of consequences of nuclear war—physical, atmospheric, ecological, agricultural, and social—Thompson and Schneider observe that the lingering effects of nuclear war, though perhaps reduced in absolute terms from earlier scenarios, could be quite severe.[16] While "apocalyptic" scenarios are regarded by the authors as improbable, they urge that such environmental effects not again be seen as "secondary."[17] An important recent study conducted under the auspices of the U.S. National Academy of Sciences concluded that, taking into account existing gaps in knowledge and methodological uncertainty, there exists a "clear possibility that great portions of the land area of the northern temperate zone (and, perhaps, a larger segment of the planet) could be severely affected" by the nuclear winter phenomenon.[18] The Department of Defense's own reports on the nuclear winter theory concur. "Even with widely ranging and unpredictable weather," the main Pentagon report on the subject concluded, "the destructiveness for human survival of the less severe climatic effects might be of a scale similar to

---

volumes, op. cit.; the report of the U.S. National Academy of Sciences, *The Effects on the Atmosphere of a Major Nuclear Exchange* (Washington, D.C.: National Academy Press, 1985); and Starley L. Thompson and Stephen H. Schneider, "Nuclear Winter Reappraised," *Foreign Affairs*, Summer 1986, pp. 981–1005. See also the authors' reply to comments in ibid., Fall 1986, pp. 171–178.

15. Thompson and Schneider, op. cit., Summer 1986, pp. 989, 998–999.
16. Ibid., pp. 990, 996–999.
17. Ibid., p. 983. For a popular account of recent work in this field, see James Gleick, "Less Drastic Theory Emerges on Freezing After a Nuclear War," *The New York Times*, June 22, 1986, pp. 1, 20. For a very skeptical account, see George W. Rathjens and Ronald H. Siegel, "Nuclear Winter: Strategic Significance," *Issues in Science and Technology*, Winter 1985, pp. 123–128.
18. *The Effects on the Atmosphere of a Major Nuclear Exchange* (Washington, D.C.: National Academy Press, 1985), p. 6.

the other horrors associated with nuclear war." "(I)f the climatic effect is severe," the report goes on, "the impact on the surviving population and biosphere could be correspondingly severe."[19]

A broad scientific consensus has thus emerged that "nuclear winter" is a scientific and socially important problem, even if, as Schneider notes, " 'global Gotterdammerung' is not a likely outcome."[20] At the same time, a great deal of public controversy has surrounded the theory, as certain advocates and opponents of the theory have sought to draw premature policy conclusions from work in progress. A number of opponents of the theory have argued that scientists working on nuclear winter, most prominently Dr. Carl Sagan, have exaggerated the significance of nuclear winter research in order to promote a specific disarmament program.[21] True, early publicized versions of the nuclear winter theory often lost sight of the scientific context in which research was being carried out, and failed to emphasize properly the methodological uncertainties and qualifications fully admitted by Sagan and his colleagues in their scientific writings. In fact, however, the progression of nuclear winter research from the relatively simple calculations of 1983/1984—reflecting available computer and modeling sophistication—to the more complex calculations of today, indicates not a refutation of the theory of nuclear winter but its confirmation and refinement in the course of normal scientific evolution.[22] Interestingly, those critics who invoke the latest work by Thompson and Schneider as refutation of the theory, have in turn been rebuked by the latter for having distorted the essential continuity in the line of research on nuclear winter.[23]

The scientific consensus behind the validity of a significant nuclear winter effect—upheld by the National Academy of Sciences and the Department of Defense—is thus impressive indeed. Whatever

---

19. Caspar W. Weinberger, Secretary of Defense, *The Potential Effects of Nuclear War on the Climate*. A Report to the United States Congress. March 1985. *Congressional Record*, March 6, 1985, p. S 2583. These conclusions were confirmed in the Pentagon's 1986 "Technical Issues Update," submitted to the Senate Armed Services Committee on May 9, 1986.
20. Letter to *The Wall Street Journal*, November 25, 1986.
21. See especially Russell Seitz, "The Melting of 'Nuclear Winter'," *The Wall Street Journal*, November 5, 1986 and Brad Sparks, "Lysenko's Ghost. The Scandal of Nuclear Winter," *National Review*, November 15, 1985, pp. 28–38.
22. Schneider, *The Wall Street Journal*, op. cit.
23. See Thompson and Schneider's correspondence in *Foreign Affairs*, op. cit., and Schneider, *Wall Street Journal*, op. cit.

the inevitable adjustments in the calculations for nuclear winter over time, two points are worth keeping in mind: first, that the hypothesis represents a plausible picture of the outcome of nuclear war; and second, that even the "best-case" scenarios, which envisage a minimal winter effect, would have catastrophic consequences for such delicate socio-ecological systems as agriculture. A few hours of temperature below some critical level would be enough to destroy certain vital crops—e.g., subfreezing for wheat, or 50–59 degrees Fahrenheit for rice.[24] A seven degree Fahrenheit (four degrees Celsius) temperature decline over a growing season is sufficient to destroy all Canadian (and Soviet) wheat and barley. A "moderate" 18 degree Fahrenheit decline, Sagan points out, is the average temperature difference between contemporary conditions and the Wisconsin Ice Age, ten to twenty thousand years ago.[25] It is hardly necessary to posit the worst case to see that the climatic and associated consequences of a "mild" nuclear winter are bad enough.

■ Impact on Deterrence

Many scientists are advancing the nuclear winter theory as the decisive argument against the arms race and in favor of nuclear disarmament. Pentagon theorists, as we have seen, have also taken note of the theory. They appear concerned about its implications for war plans that necessarily encompass the large-scale bombing of cities and about possible public reaction against the U.S. military posture were the theory to gain broad public acceptance. Yet it is not immediately apparent why the nuclear winter theory should arouse the passion and interest it does. If, disregarding the nuclear winter effect, nuclear war already poses the certainty of unacceptable damage to U.S. and Soviet societies, it would then merely emphasize the mutual horror of nuclear war and thus enhance deterrence, as, indeed, some have argued. Others seem more concerned about the effect of nuclear winter on U.S. ability to prosecute future nuclear wars. For example, Rand analyst J.J. Gertler, in a paper entitled "Some Policy Implications of Nuclear Winter," wrote that:

---

24. Thompson and Schneider, op. cit., p. 996.
25. Carl Sagan, comment to *Foreign Affairs*, Fall 1986, pp. 164–165.

Following the onset of nuclear winter and through its duration, such optical reconnaissance satellites (and SDI system sensors) as survived countermeasures during the exchange will be effectively blinded as soot fills the Earth's atmosphere. The lack of light will also sharply reduce the imaging ability of airborne cameras (as well as interfering with the propulsion systems of recon aircraft). Infrared sources will be more easily detected because of their contrast with the cooling atmosphere, but could well be masked by the massive fires generated by the exchange. We may have to develop alternative intelligence-gathering measures, particularly to detect long-term delayed launches from reloadable silos. Also, the erosion and friction effects of an upper-altitude soot layer on outbound missiles—possibly causing damage and/or gross inaccuracy—must be evaluated.[26]

In fact, the nuclear winter theory represents *both* an essential continuity in the nuclear era and something altogether new.

By introducing the probability of yet another catastrophic result of nuclear war, the nuclear winter theory simply reinforces the basic truth of the nuclear age: that nuclear weapons have no useful military function except to deter others from using theirs. Even during the period of crushing U.S. strategic superiority, American leaders did not find their scenarios for nuclear warfighting very persuasive. The certainty that at least several million Americans would die as the consequence of a nuclear war was sufficient in 1961 to convince Paul Nitze that U.S. plans for nuclear escalation in the event of an explosion of the Berlin crisis were utterly unrealistic.[27] The general horror provoked by the outcome of the "Carte Blanche" war games in 1955, in which one and a half million civilian deaths were predicted following the use of battlefield nuclear weapons in West Germany, contrasts starkly with the equanimity of strategic discourse today when the minimum casualties (from primary, short-term effects alone) of a nuclear war between the superpowers are estimated to begin in the scores of million. So, it should not take nuclear winter to persuade planners and leaders that nuclear war is a very special kind of hell. By all available evidence they are already convinced that it would be.

---

26. J.J. Gertler, *Some Policy Implications of Nuclear Winter* (Washington, D.C.: The Rand Corporation, January 1985), p. 13. See also Philip J. Romero, "Nuclear Winter: Implications for U.S. and Soviet Nuclear Strategy," *The Rand Paper Series*, no. P-7009-RGI, December 1984.

27. Fred Kaplan, *Wizards of Armageddon* (New York: Simon and Schuster, 1983), pp. 300–301.

In another sense, however, the nuclear winter theory appears to challenge nuclear deterrence in a unique way. The point becomes clearer if we consider that nuclear deterrence really has two aspects. *First*, there is the deterrent effect produced by the sheer existence of nuclear weapons. The simple possession of these weapons by a state (assuming the invulnerability of a portion of its forces) would appear to exert a deterrent influence, independent of whether that state has developed an elaborate doctrine for the use of such weapons and integrated the weapons and doctrine into its military and foreign policies. The credibility of one's deterrent is not an issue in this case. Even an extremely low possibility of an event with infinitely catastrophic consequences (such as nuclear war)—and such a possibility can never be excluded as long as nuclear weapons exist—would appear to be most convincing in dissuading any rational actor from undertaking actions that might lead to such an eventuality. The deterrence that is obtained in these circumstances might be termed "existential deterrence," since the deterrent effect is inherent in the very existence of nuclear weapons. The nuclear winter phenomenon, in this context, simply adds one more horrifying consequence to what is already recognized to be an unacceptably horrible possibility and so only reinforces, if that is indeed possible, the effectiveness of this existential deterrence.

The *second* aspect of deterrence is related to the fact that military planners and politicians have never felt completely comfortable with the logic of existential deterrence, widely known under the term "mutual assured destruction." A government attempting to incorporate nuclear weapons into its military and foreign policy must plan for the possible use of such weapons, developing scenarios in which, *in extremis*, a country's political interests can be furthered by the use of such weapons, and make the threat (to a potential foe) or promise (to allies) to use nuclear weapons plausible. This second aspect of nuclear deterrence, "deterrence as doctrine," then, unlike existential deterrence, presupposes some degree of military-operational credibility in nuclear force planning and doctrine. Such credibility need not be very high. As I have said, even a small possibility of an infinitely large catastrophe should suffice to deter a rational opponent. Yet if a state is trying to pursue a range of foreign policy objectives beyond national survival on the basis of nuclear deterrence, particularly if these involve the reassurance of allies as well as the deterrence of potential enemies, then a certain degree of military-operational credibility appears essential to the effectiveness of one's nuclear deterrent and, consequently, to the foreign policies dependent on it. That is the deterrent function of war planning. Such planning, and the doctrines that accompany it, may be highly improbable. Indeed, much of the political tension surrounding the enunciation and elaboration of nuclear doctrine would seem to derive from the effort to make the inherently implausible—i.e., the threat (or promise) to use weapons whose implementation would almost certainly be suicidal—believable. Yet however low the credibility of such a policy, the effectiveness of deterrent doctrine demands that it not be nil. The possibility of "victory," in the sense of attaining politically significant goals through nuclear use, must not in principle be excluded.

By all evidence, Western politicians have not been much impressed with the utility of the various nuclear alternatives before them. It is difficult to conceive of circumstances, at least in the East-West context, in which one side could advance its political interests through the actual employment of nuclear weapons. Yet it has at least been possible for politicians and force planners to develop scenarios in which, depending on the response of the adversary, one might emerge better off having used nuclear weapons. Thus the NATO strategy of the possible first-use of nuclear weapons remains in effect.

It is here, in its impact on "deterrence as doctrine," that the nuclear winter theory would appear to exert its greatest effect. Until now, "victory" in a nuclear war merely seemed impossible to attain in light of the prevailing balance of terror. If, however, a sufficient degree of unilateral superiority could be achieved, then the opponent might be effectively disarmed and one could emerge from a nuclear war having suffered only "acceptable" damage. The *concept*, at least, of nuclear victory, could thus be preserved. But the effect of the nuclear winter theory on planners reverses this logic: *even if one side achieves a perfectly disarming first strike*, he might thereby bring devastation down upon himself by triggering nuclear winter and associated long-term effects. Thus, the nuclear winter concept goes to the heart of extended deterrence doctrine: by highlighting the possibly suicidal consequences of even the "successful" use of nuclear weapons, the theory tends to undermine the credibility of deterrence as a consciously formulated military and foreign-policy doctrine and therefore of any policy depending directly upon it.

Seen in another way, the advent of nuclear weapons was viewed—before the development of the nuclear winter hypothesis—as providing the possibility of annihilating one's opponent without having defeated his armed forces. This was really only an extension of the capabilities inherent in strategic bombing, as the bombing of Germany and Japan during the Second World War showed. The implications of the nuclear winter theory are far more radical, for they suggest that, even if one side had decisively defeated the armed forces of one's opponent, it might in the process have laid the seeds for the devastation of its own society. If that is so, or merely plausibly so, it would appear to remove the fangs from any posture of extended nuclear deterrence, dependent as it is on a finite degree of operational military efficacy.

On the other hand, one might argue that the nuclear winter effect constitutes a kind of natural "doomsday machine," the device conjured up by Herman Kahn and made famous by the film "Dr. Strangelove" which, by promising the automatic destruction of the world in the wake of a nuclear attack, becomes the foolproof deterrent.[28] Credibility is not a factor in this kind of deterrent, since the system is completely automatic: furthermore, any effort to dismantle the system sets it off. Certainly the nuclear winter phenomenon may be viewed as a sort of natural doomsday machine (even if the ultimate effect is less than apocalyptic), and so the ultimate deterrent. In this view, nuclear winter need not compel any changes in our nuclear policies since the U.S. policy of deterrence, by supposedly preventing nuclear war, thereby also prevents nuclear winter. Anything which heightens the costs an enemy will pay in a nuclear war is thus to be welcomed, and is viewed as entirely consistent with U.S. policy. Richard Perle, Assistant Secretary of Defense for International Security Affairs, thus told two House subcommittees on March 14, 1985: "We believe what we are doing with respect to strategic doctrine and arms control is basically sound and our acceptance of the nuclear winter theory does not make it less sound. . . . There is no shred of evidence," Perle continued, "that our current doctrine is not the best policy to prevent nuclear war."[29]

There are a number of objections to this line of reasoning. First, even Herman Kahn opposed the creation of a "doomsday machine" because it was simply too automatic, leaving no room for human

---

28. Herman Kahn, *On Thermonuclear War* (New York: The Free Press, 1969), pp. 145–149.
29. Reuters dispatch, March 14, 1985; Associated Press dispatch, March 15, 1985.

choice. Unlike the "doomsday machine" of Kahn's imagination, however, the natural doomsday effect constituted by nuclear winter can be dismantled through human choice. Man has the capacity of removing this threat to himself by reducing his stockpile of nuclear weapons below the minimum "threshold" (as difficult as that may be to determine) deemed necessary to induce nuclear winter. Nuclear winter is not an immutable law of the universe; it comes into effect only through willful human intervention. It therefore follows that such intervention can remove the threat.

Second, even if one accepted the contention that nuclear winter simply reinforces the existing policy of deterrence, it would be necessary to point out that the U.S. government, as well as the USSR, is spending immense sums of money to maintain nuclear forces far above the levels needed to induce the catastrophe said to enhance deterrence (depending on the scenario employed, possibly several hundred megatons, compared to the approximately 13,000 megatons contained in the nearly 50,000 nuclear weapons fielded by the U.S. and USSR). That these sums continue to be spent—in light of the Pentagon's own recognition of the validity of the theory—suggests either actual skepticism as to the soundness of the theory or a deep-rooted conceptual conservatism. It would appear that, visions of Reykjavik notwithstanding, the leaders of the nuclear superpowers envision nothing better than the continuation of the system of nuclear deterrence, resting as it does on the threat of mass annihilation. Unfortunately, the elegance of deterrence theory hinges upon a finite possibility that this implicit threat will have to be implemented. And the nuclear winter hypothesis highlights not simply the inexpediency of such a policy (through loss of military-operational credibility) but the very real threat to civilization itself.

One may object: but if a less credible, non-nuclear deterrent fails and erupts into war, who can say that nuclear weapons will not be used? To which the answer is: such a guarantee cannot be given, which is why the capacity to obliterate civilization that is inherent in the present disposition of nuclear weapons must be dismantled.

These general conclusions, of course, presume the soundness of the nuclear winter theory. As indicated above, there have been a number of challenges made to the scientific basis on which the theory has been built. Most scientists working on the theory openly admit the range of uncertainty in estimating such complex, multidimensional meteorological processes involved in modeling the nuclear winter theory.³⁰ Yet the exact possibility of the theory itself—90 percent, 60 percent, 20 percent, 5 percent—and the prewar intentions of politicians are largely irrelevant here (though the challenges to the theory's fundamental validity have so far been successfully answered). As for the latter, as Albert Wohlstetter notes, the history of warfare points to "the uncertain evolution of sequences likely in real contingencies."³¹ As for the former, and this is what is really unique about the theory of nuclear winter, the issue is now the degree of probability of the virtual extinction of human civilization. The nuclear winter theory provides a plausible forecast of how this may come about. In that case, does it really matter whether the degree of probability is 9 in 10 or 1 in 20? Of course, no one can predict with certainty that, in the event of a nuclear war, nuclear winter will be touched off. But—and this is the real point—no one can say with any degree of confidence that it will not. Furthermore, even were the nuclear winter theory to be completely disproven (unlikely, except in the actual event of nuclear war), there would still remain the probability of other, unforeseeable and potentially catastrophic long-term consequences of nuclear warfare (in addition to the horrific short *and* long-term effects already known). As the nuclear winter study conducted by the U.S. National Academy of Sciences concluded, "One can ask whether even now the full range of physical consequences—let alone the biological effects—of nuclear warfare is within our comprehension."³²

While a number of academic defense analysts have criticized the modeling done to test the nuclear winter theory for worrying about "the wrong sorts of wars," as Thomas Powers put it, U.S. defense officials have not shared their skepticism.³³ Unlike outside theorists, U.S. strategic planners are all too aware that "all versions of the SIOP (Single Integrated Operational Plan) include plans for a society-destroying attack on Soviet 'recovery targets'—the Soviet institutions that make Russia strong—and thousands of these targets are in Soviet

---

30. See, for example, *Effects on the Atmosphere*, op. cit., "Preface," pp. 1, 5–6; Aleksandr S. Ginzburg, " 'Yadernaya Zima'—Real'naya Ugroza Chelovechestvu" ("Nuclear Winter"—A Real Threat to Mankind), *S.Sh.A.* (Moscow), no. 3 (March 1985), pp. 53, 58–59.
31. Wohlstetter, op. cit., p. 977.
32. *Effects on the Atmosphere*, op. cit., p. 187.
33. Thomas Powers, "Nuclear Winter and Nuclear Strategy," *The Atlantic Monthly*, November 1984, p. 58.

cities."³⁴ "If those (high priority) targets are attacked," Powers notes, "the cities will burn. If these targets are spared, we have no theory of how to fight a nuclear war."³⁵ Defense planners thus have every reason to take the nuclear winter hypothesis seriously. Yet, in the previously cited report in which the Defense Department accepted the validity of the nuclear winter theory, it was quick to add that the theory had no significant implications for U.S. policy.³⁶ Such a conclusion is comprehensible in the sense that, by adding to the manifest of horrors associated with nuclear war, nuclear winter emphasizes the unacceptability, and thus improbability (though not impossibility) of nuclear war. "Existential deterrence," as it has been portrayed, would be enhanced; indeed, the requirements for maintaining its effectiveness may even be said to have been reduced. Yet the particular way in which the nuclear winter theory erodes "deterrence as doctrine"—by undermining, through its "boomerang" effect, the plausibility of military-operational options for the use of nuclear weapons—challenges efforts to integrate nuclear weapons into a military and foreign policy extending beyond territorial defense. Indeed, it is the basic thesis of this paper, to be detailed in Part 3, that the nuclear winter hypothesis implies far-reaching conclusions for operational planning for the possible use of nuclear weapons.

---

34. Ibid., p. 60. While the Strategic Air Command no longer targets cities "per se," the "Single Integrated Operational Plan" (SIOP-5D) includes 15,000 industrial and economic targets in the USSR and Eastern Europe. These include (a) war-supporting industries, ammunition factories, tank and armored personnel factories, petroleum facilities, railway yards, and repair facilities; and (b) industries that contribute to economic recovery—coal, basic steel, basic aluminums, and electric power. The objective, in the final analysis, is to be able to destroy 70 percent of the Soviet industry deemed necessary to achieve postwar economic "recovery." The SIOP also includes 2,000 military and political leadership targets. Most of these targets are located in or quite close to cities. Peter Pringle and William Arkin, *SIOP: The Secret U.S. Plan for Nuclear War* (New York: Norton, 1983), pp. 183, 186–187, 191–192. While Moscow *as such* may not be targeted, the SIOP includes sixty targets inside of Moscow. Joseph S. Nye, Jr., "Nuclear Winter and Policy Choices," *Survival*, March/April, 1986, p. 222. See also Desmond Ball, "Toward a Critique of Strategic Nuclear Targeting," in Desmond Ball and Jeffrey Richelson (eds.), *Strategic Nuclear Targeting* (Ithaca: Cornell University Press, 1986), pp. 27–28; idem., "The Development of the SIOP, 1960–1983," in ibid., pp. 79–80; and Jeffrey Richelson, "Population Targeting and U.S. Strategic Doctrine," ibid., pp. 234–249.
35. Powers, op. cit., p. 63.
36. Op. cit., pp. S2583–S2585.

2

"Nuclear Winter" and the Soviet Union

Some observers have worried that if the West persuaded itself of the validity of the nuclear winter theory while the Soviet Union remained unconvinced, great danger might thereby result for the West. Rand analyst Gertler, for example, believes that "any government that does not take the threat of nuclear winter seriously will be less restrained in its nuclear-arms policies than one that does, as it might believe that a nuclear war might be fought and won. Symmetry of belief is important . . . [otherwise] they could become more aggressive, gambling that we are too afraid of initiating a nuclear winter to respond."[37]

Certainly, every effort should be made so that Soviet and American leaders come to a common understanding on the validity of the theory of nuclear winter and its implications for their mutual relations and military postures. And it is true that Soviet disbelief in the possibility of nuclear winter would tend to frustrate transition to the radically denuclearized world that the nuclear winter hypothesis seems to imply. This does not mean, though, that Soviet rejection of the theory would present the United States and its allies with threats they do not already face.

In the first place, there are a number of measures which the United States and its allies should take unilaterally, irrespective of the Soviet attitude, in order to improve their own security and reduce the threat of nuclear winter. Since, as I have argued, the prospect of nuclear winter represents as much a continuation of the basic logic of

---

37. Gertler, op. cit., p. 16. See also Francis P. Hoeber and Robert K. Squire, "The 'Nuclear Winter' Hypothesis: Some Policy Implications," *Strategic Review*, Summer 1985, pp. 44.

the nuclear age—i.e., that nuclear weapons' sole function is to prevent others from using theirs—as a departure from it, certain problems will persist independently of the Soviet position on nuclear winter. These include an alliance strategy envisioning the possible first-use of nuclear arms and a strategic targeting doctrine which, if fully implemented, could lead to the onset of nuclear winter. Nuclear winter simply highlights the incredibility of an American nuclear guarantee to Western Europe, a guarantee that the condition of mutual assured destruction—by drawing attention to the suicidal character of this nuclear promise—called into question long ago. Even if the theory of nuclear winter could be disproven (which it can not, short of nuclear war), the implausibility of this promise would remain, with all of its attendant political consequences. Soviet assent to the theory of nuclear winter would not change the essence of that problem.

Furthermore, Soviet rejection of the nuclear winter theory need not enhance the capacity of the USSR to engage in "nuclear blackmail." Since the key to blackmail is to be found in the psychological vulnerability of the intended victim, Western acceptance of the nuclear winter theory itself would provide a sure shield against such pressures. If the West were convinced of its position, Soviet nuclear threats would be deprived of all credibility, since in the Western mind the USSR would suffer, through the boomerang effect induced by nuclear winter, damage out of all proportion to any political goal it could achieve through execution of such a threat.*

Secondly, Soviet politicians and military leaders do not need a theory of nuclear winter to remind them that the consequences of nuclear war would be horrible beyond all previous historical experience and imagination. Since the twentieth party congress in 1956, Soviet foreign policy has been predicated upon the assumption that nuclear war would mean utter devastation for socialism and capitalism alike. Indeed, a dispute about this very issue was one of the underlying reasons for the Sino-Soviet split, causing the USSR to lose its major ally. This thesis was reinforced and made more explicit during the 1970s, as Leonid Brezhnev consolidated his authority and imposed the

---

*Independent of the nuclear winter phenomenon, nuclear blackmail would appear a highly improbable, because implausible, undertaking. If he chooses to execute his threat, the blackmailer/aggressor would be leaving the issue of his own survival entirely in the hands of his recent victim, through the latter's choice of a retaliatory strike. No country, and least of all the USSR, has been known to behave so imprudently.

doctrine—in the face of reservations by some in the military—that there could be no winners in a nuclear war.[38] Countless Soviet foreign-policy analysts, writing for each other, have observed that thermonuclear weapons, by having "introduced qualitative changes in the posing of the question of war and peace in the contemporary world," have eliminated the choice of general war as a means of attaining political objectives. The son of former Politburo member Viktor Grishin wrote in 1982 of "the impossibility of preserving the institution of military victory in an unlimited, global, nuclear missile war. ... This changes the historical and political evaluation of war as such."[39] The late Nikolai Inozemtsev, former Director of the prestigious Institute of World Economy and International Relations, held that nuclear warfare is "fraught with the annihilation of the very conditions of human existence."[40] This "compels us all," one Soviet observer noted in the popular weekly *Literaturnaya Gazeta*, "to new conceptions."[41]

It is clear, therefore, that Soviet observers, and leaders, view the consequences of nuclear war—independent of the probability of nuclear winter—with the utmost sobriety and concern. Furthermore, there is no evidence that the Soviet Union has rejected the plausibility of the nuclear winter theory and much to indicate that it takes the prospect quite seriously. A number of skeptical voices, though, have been raised on this score. The Pentagon report formally accepting the validity of the nuclear winter theory maintained that Soviet researchers "have done little original work on the subject and show no evidence of regarding the whole matter as anything more than an opportunity for propaganda."[42] Richard Turco, co-author of the original "nuclear winter" article published in *Science* magazine in De-

---

38. See Raymond Garthoff's analysis in "Detente and Military Doctrine," in *Detente and Confrontation: American-Soviet Relations From Nixon to Reagan* (Washington, D.C.: Brookings Institution, 1985), pp. 768–785.
39. N.M. Nikol'sky and A.V. Grishin, *Nauchno-teknichesky progress i mezhdunarodnye otnosheniya* (Scientific-technical Progress and International Relations) (Moscow: Mezhdunarodnye Otnosheniya, 1978), pp. 42, 47, 56, 263; idem., *Sistemny analiz i dialog s EVM v issledovanii mezhdunarodnykh otnoshenii* (Systems Analysis and the Dialogue with the Computer in Research on International Relations) (Moscow: Mezhdunarodnye Otnosheniya, 1982), p. 35.
40. N.N. Inozemtsev, "Policy of Peaceful Coexistence: Underlying Principles," in *Soviet Policy of Peace* (Moscow: Social Sciences Today, 1979), p. 6.
41. Remark by Vladimir Lomeiko in *Literaturnaya Gazeta*, August 29, 1979.
42. Op. cit., p. S2583.

cember 1983, has charged that the climate model presented by Dr. Vladimir Aleksandrov of the Soviet Academy of Sciences in support of the nuclear winter hypothesis was "a very weak piece of work, crude and seriously flawed . . . (actually) a primitive rendition of an obsolete U.S. model."[43] Turco contends that "the Soviets have contributed little to the international 'nuclear winter' study effort thus far, and quite a few people are extremely disappointed."[44]

It is interesting that all of the U.S. criticisms of the Soviet research effort on nuclear winter have focused on the *relative* unsophistication (i.e., relative to the U.S.) of the models the Soviets have been able to develop. No one has claimed that the Soviets are not doing work in this field; rather, critics charge that the work that is being done does not display the technical virtuosity expected by American scientists. Now the virtuosity that American scientists have been able to display in elaborating the theory of nuclear winter is in large measure due to the models they have been able to develop. These models, in turn, depend on the sophistication of the computers that are available to test them. Without an extremely high level of computer development it is not possible to derive the kinds of detailed conclusions reached by the American theorists of nuclear winter. A 1966 Rand report on "The Effects of Nuclear War on the Weather and Climate" examined the possible effects of smoke and soot on the earth's climate and concluded that, while such effects would certainly make themselves felt, the methodological basis for predicting them in detail simply did not exist.[45] Given the generally acknowledged lag in Soviet computer development, it is possible that Soviet scientists have been facing similar methodological difficulties. In fact, Soviet scientists working on the nuclear winter theory openly admit the greater technical sophistication of the models their American colleagues have been working with.[46] This, in turn, might explain the recent series of Soviet

---

43. *Science*, July 6, 1984, p. 31.
44. Ibid. Leon Goure makes the same point in " 'Nuclear Winter' in Soviet Mirrors," *Strategic Review*, Summer 1985, pp. 23–38.
45. E.S. Batten, *The Effects of Nuclear War on the Weather and Climate*, op. cit., p. 44, passim.
46. Ginzburg, "Yadernaya Zima," op. cit., p. 55; Georgi Stenchikov, "Climatic Consequences of Nuclear War. Computational Experiments with the Hydrodynamic Model of the Computing Center of the USSR Academy of Sciences," in Yevgeny Velikhov (ed.), *The Night After* (Moscow: Mir Publishers, 1985), p. 56; see comments by Georgi Golitsyn and Vladimir Aleksandrov in Paul R. Ehrlich et al. (eds.), *The Cold and the Dark. The World After Nuclear War* (New York: Norton, 1984), pp. 87, 96; 103–104, respectively.

requests—turned down by the U.S. government—to employ U.S. "supercomputers" to test the theory of nuclear winter.[47]

The additional charge raised by American skeptics is that the USSR is only interested in exploiting the nuclear theory for propaganda purposes. Certainly, there is a potential for the political exploitation of the nuclear winter theory. It is also true that the USSR has exploited and will continue to exploit all such opportunities as are available to it.[48] True but also not to the point. Insofar as nuclear winter reinforces the political disutility of all nuclear threats, it reinforces the incredibility of policies resting on that threat: *reinforces*, but not creates. The question of devising a credible military and foreign policy is the central issue. It is the condition of mutual destruction through assured retaliation that has posed the main challenge to an active nuclear deterrent doctrine. Nuclear winter is, in a sense, simply the highest expression of this condition; with nuclear winter, destruction (or "unacceptable damage") may be assured even without retaliation. It hardly requires a theory of nuclear winter to afford the USSR the occasion to exploit the vulnerabilities of an incredible U.S. nuclear guarantee to Western Europe.

Furthermore, the scientific discussion on the effects of nuclear war on the climate reveals that a fraction of the probable nuclear winter effect is sufficient to cause temperatures in the northern hemisphere to drop an average of two to three degrees Celsius, more than

---

47. As reported in *The New York Times*, August 17, 1985, p. 9, and February 10, 1986, p. A13.
48. Examples of Soviet exploitation of the nuclear winter theory include: the connection between the theory and no-first-use of nuclear weapons made by Academician Yevgeny Velikhov, Vice-President of the USSR Academy of Sciences, in *Literaturnaya Gazeta*, January 22, 1986, p. 14—Velikhov stresses that "the possibility of being the first to use nuclear weapons . . . is the pivot of all U.S. political and military doctrine." See also Velikhov's introduction to *The Night After*, op. cit., in which he attempts to demonstrate how the nuclear winter theory supports Soviet arms control policy (focusing on the Strategic Defense Initiative), pp. 22–32; and a TASS dispatch in English, January 13, 1986 along the same lines, cited in Foreign Broadcast Information Service (FBIS), *Daily Report: Soviet Union—National Affairs*, January 14, 1986, p. u1. A particularly egregious instance is the statement by Nikita Moiseyev, Deputy Director of the Computing Center of the Soviet Academy of Sciences, cited by TASS, that "[a]n effect, similar to the 'nuclear winter' one, might also emerge as a result of the use of conventional weapons whose capacity is constantly increasing." The statement was made to *New Times*, a heavily propagandistic Soviet weekly with widespread translation and distribution around the world. Moscow TASS in English, 1330 GMT, February 28, 1986, in *FBIS Daily Report: Soviet Union*, March 5, 1986, p. AA3.

enough to make agriculture in a northern country such as the USSR impossible. In other words, the USSR would be among the very first countries to suffer immeasurable and possibly irreversible catastrophe even with the minimum, or "best-case" scenarios posited by the nuclear winter theory. With their daily experience of the vagaries of the weather, and the cruel effect exerted on its agriculture, the Soviet authorities would certainly be most sensitive to this fact.[49]

In fact, an examination of expressed Soviet views on the nuclear winter hypothesis reveals that the Soviets are quite receptive to the general message implicit in the concept. A number of joint Soviet-American conferences have been held to discuss the ramifications of the theory. These have been broadcast on Soviet television.[50] A number of commentaries on the nuclear winter theory have been published in the Soviet press. No doubt, the USSR discovered with the controversies over the "neutron bomb" and NATO INF deployments that all things nuclear have become a neuralgic point in Western bodies politic. Since the primary military goal of Soviet policy in Europe is to neutralize the nuclear foundation NATO's strategy, the USSR can be expected to press every possibility for stirring controversy over nuclear issues in Western public opinion. The increasing prominence of the nuclear winter theory in the West would thus present the USSR with a natural channel for pursuing its propaganda offensive against NATO policy. Nevertheless, the message in Soviet commentary on the nuclear winter theory is invariably the same, whether the audience is foreign or Soviet, the masses or specialists: the threat of nuclear winter is real.

The methodological foundation for Soviet research into the nuclear winter effect was laid by a climate model developed in the mid-1970s at the Computing Center of the USSR Academy of Sciences to simulate small-scale changes of climate brought about by man-made effects on the climate system and evaluate their ecological and economic implications.[51] The Soviet Computing Center began its

---

49. Ernest A. Bondietii, "Effects on Agriculture," *Ambio*, op. cit., pp. 138–142; Howard W. Hjort, "The Impact on Global Food Supplies," Ibid., pp. 153–157; and Janet Raloff, "Nuclear Winter: Shutting Down the Farm?" *Science News*, September 14, 1985, pp. 171–173. See also Thompson and Schneider, op. cit., p. 1004.
50. Moscow television, in Russian, July 16, 1985, 1510 GMT, and March 24, 1984, 1440 GMT, broadcast conferences in which, inter alia, the astronomer Carl Sagan expounded his work on nuclear winter to Soviet television audiences.
51. Stenchikov, "Climatic Consequences of Nuclear War. Computational Experiments," op. cit., p. 54.

research of the climatic consequences of nuclear war in early 1983, shortly after Crutzen and Birks published their findings in the Swedish journal *Ambio* on the effects of the smoke produced by forest fires ignited by a massive nuclear war.[52] The objective was "to calculate the long-term major fluctuations in the climate system" following the injection of aerosol, soot, smoke, and chemical by-products after a large-scale nuclear war.[53]

The Soviet scientists used a three-dimensional, hydrodynamic model, employing as extreme cases 100-megaton ("countervalue") and 10,000-megaton (mixed targeting) nuclear war scenarios. The conclusions reached by the Soviet scientists, derived independently and from different methodologies than those used by their Western colleagues, essentially coincide with findings reached so far by Western scientists:

> Nuclear explosions would start off massive fires that would be attended by vast amounts of atmospheric combustion products—soot, ashes and noxious gases. Clouds of fine soot particles would absorb and scatter sunlight to cause a pall of darkness over the earth's surface, or a 'nuclear night'. Thus the planet's radiation balance would be upset and within a short time interval the surface temperatures would be lowered by 20–50°C below the seasonal norm. Such an abrupt cooling would set up a 'nuclear winter' even in the summer season and, following a fundamental restructuring of the atmospheric circulation system, this unprecedented climatic catastrophe would spread in a matter of a few weeks all over the globe to cause massive death among the Earth's flora and fauna.[54]

---

52. Op. cit.
53. Stenchikov, op. cit., pp. 55–56. For a detailed description of the model employed, see ibid., pp. 56–60.
54. Yevgeny Velikhov, "Introduction," in idem, *The Night After*, op. cit., pp. 7–8. For confirmation of this finding by other Soviet scientists, see the contributions by meteorologist Yury Izrael, mathematician Georgi Stenchikov, and atmospheric physicists Georgi Golitsyn and Aleksandr Ginzburg in Ibid., pp. 37–98, respectively. This important volume, which contains the methodologies used by Soviet scientists to test the nuclear winter theory, was published in Russian as *Noch' Posle* (Moscow: Nauka, 1985). See also the studies by Ginzburg, "Yadernaya Zima," op. cit.; physicist Sergei Kapitsa, "Nauchit'sya Dumat' Po-Novomu" (Learning to Think in New Categories), *Inostrannaya Literatura*, no. 1 (January 1986), pp. 199–206, a translation and expansion of "Global Consequences of a Nuclear War and the World After," *Disarmament*, vol. VIII, no. 1, 1985; see also the Soviet contributions to Ehrlich et al. (eds.), *The Cold and the Dark*, op. cit., passim, as well as the account of the theory given by Yury Fyodorov, "'Yadernaya zima' i yadernyi kurs S.Sh.A." ("Nuclear Winter" and U.S. Nuclear Policy), *Mirovaya Ekonomika i Mezhdunarodnye Otnosheniya*, no. 6 (June 1986), pp. 77–82.

The discussion of nuclear winter in the USSR has not been limited to specialists, as often happens with controversial issues. Mass audiences in the Soviet Union have been told that "Recent scientific investigations demonstrate cogently that nuclear war could trigger uncontrollable climatic and other environmental changes over huge regions of the earth."[55] A detailed report in *Izvestiya*, the official newspaper of the Soviet government, spoke of "new factors" to consider in the discussion of the effects of nuclear war: these were "factors of global changes in the climate." "According to the latest estimates," the article went on to say:

> the utilization of even a small part of the nuclear weapons stockpile will entail a sharp and prolonged drop in temperature which will affect the entire globe and which means that the geophysical consequences of nuclear war will be considerably more harmful than the immediate effect of nuclear weapons.

Referring to the scientific work that had taken place in the United States, the Soviet Union, and West Germany, the article stated:

> The authors of the various calculations agree in all their main conclusions, which provides the best proof of their objectivity. These conclusions are so grave and important that they have become the subject of widespread discussion and detailed critical analysis.[56]

No doubt much of the substantive research in the Soviet Union on the probability and consequences of nuclear winter is taking place under the auspices of the military and is therefore classified. (Ironically, the study being undertaken for the U.S. Defense Nuclear Agency on Soviet views of the nuclear winter phenomenon, written by Science Applications, Inc., is itself classified.[57]) The sharp barriers between research with direct military application and all other research in the Soviet Union would certainly apply in the instance of work on nuclear winter, leading, perhaps, to a less than desired methodological foundation for the work of many scientists in this area. The uneven scientific quality of the Soviet paper on space-based defensive systems published in the spring of 1984 is surely not the only case of this kind.[58] A general lag in computer technology may

---

55. *Sovetskaya Rossiya*, November 30, 1984.
56. *Izvestiya*, July 25, 1984. See also ibid., July 28, 1985 and *Sotsialisticheskaya Industriya*, March 28, 1985.
57. *Science*, July 6, 1984, p. 31.
58. Based on a technical analysis given by Lt. Col. Thomas H. Johnson, Director of the Science Research Laboratory, West Point, at the Institute for East-West Security

well add to the constraints on Soviet research in this area. Indeed, Soviet physicist Sergei Kapitsa hinted at some of the difficulties Soviet scientists may have faced in a speech he gave in New York in early 1985. The alarm over nuclear winter, Kapitsa noted, "was raised first by independent academic and university scientists, not by those who came from the 'Great Secret Laboratories' for nuclear armaments. Those in secret work," Kapitsa went on to say,

> should have been the first to comprehend the full consequences of their inventions. I must admit that some did try, but they did not manage to succeed, to get their signal out of the scientific-military establishment, to make themselves heard and understood, to communicate with the body politic and the public at large. Now they are joining in this research where their professional knowledge is certainly welcome.
>
> Highly specialized scientists, working in strictly compartmentalized military research establishments, usually lack the broad understanding without which it is practically impossible to explore and work profitably on interdisciplinary problems.[59]

The sensitivity of the issue may be gauged by the fact that when Kapitsa's article was translated into Russian for publication in the Soviet press, the focus of his criticism was shifted entirely to *Western* scientists.[60] The nuclear winter issue and its implications may be considerably more controversial in the USSR than the publicly available evidence suggests. At any rate, the papers that have so far been presented, the consistency of the basic message to all audiences—foreign and domestic, specialists and masses—creates a strong presumption that Soviet scientists find the nuclear winter hypothesis a compelling one, and that they have managed to convince the Soviet leadership that the threat of nuclear winter is at least as grave as that posed by any of the other effects of nuclear war.[61]

Studies, February 19, 1985. See Roald Z. Sagdeyev and Andrei A. Kokoshin, *A Space-Based Anti-Missile System with Directed Energy Weapons: Strategic, Legal and Political Implications* (Moscow: April, 1984).

59. Kapitsa, "Global Consequences of a Nuclear War," op. cit., p. 127.
60. "I pochemu segodnya *na Zapade* trevoga byla podnyata nezavisimymi uchenymi iz akademicheskikh i universitetskikh krugov, a ne temi, kto rabotal v gigantskikh zakrytykh laboratoriyakh po sozdaniyu yadernogo oruzhiya?" [emphasis added] Kapitsa, "Nauchit'sya Dumat' Po-Novomu," op. cit., p. 205.
61. Soviet Foreign Minister Eduard Shevardnadze made a passing reference to the nuclear winter concept in his speech before the United Nations General Assembly on September 24, 1985. FBIS, *Daily Report: Soviet Union*, September 25, 1985, p. CC6.

3
Political and Military Implications

The political and military consequences of the nuclear winter theory follow from the possibility that even a disarming first strike could induce the nuclear winter effect, thereby wreaking unacceptable damage upon the initiator. If this proposition is accepted, it would tend to undermine the effectiveness of nuclear deterrence doctrine by nullifying the credibility of any nuclear threat (or promise). Policies that depend on nuclear deterrence for their effectiveness would also thereby be thrown into question. If even the militarily successful execution of the deterrent threat poses the danger of self-inflicted catastrophe, the deterrent threat/promise loses whatever residual credibility that lent it efficacy. This has immediate implications for alliance relations within both NATO and the Warsaw Pact, for the strategic weapons policies of the United States and the Soviet Union, and for arms control and disarmament policy in general.

■ Impact on Strategic Weapons Policies

The formidable strategic nuclear forces of the United States and the Soviet Union currently possess many times the destructive power estimated to create the nuclear winter effect. Many of these weapons are targeted upon cities. Others would start forest and grasslands fires that would contribute significantly to the threat of nuclear winter. Acceptance of the nuclear winter theory by the superpowers would seem to exert two interrelated effects upon their strategic weapons policies. It would raise the incentives for them first to reduce the total destructive power of their arsenals, and second to increase centralized political authority over the release of nuclear weapons and perfect their command, communications, control, and intelligence capacities for the discriminate use of those weapons. This would be aimed at insuring that, in the event of nuclear war, cities would not be hit and that, should events get out of control, neither country would have the capacity to unleash nuclear winter.

Moral considerations alone dictate that such measures be taken. Nuclear winter adds a compelling element of self-interest into the legal and moral code governing the use of weapons of mass destruction. If their nuclear deterrents are to retain any semblance of credibility as weapons of war, Soviet and American strategic forces must under no circumstances target the cities of the other country: the execution of such plans could entail the destruction of the attacking party. Furthermore, since there is always the possibility that during a crisis or war the central authorities may lose control, the combined nuclear forces of both the Soviet Union and the United States would have to be deprived of their theoretical capacity to trigger nuclear winter. This could only be done through joint effort.

A nuclear posture that would reflect the implications of nuclear winter would appear to dovetail neatly with the kind of "deliberately moral" strategy that has been urged by some critics of contemporary nuclear strategy.[62] Such a strategy would be designed, as indicated above, to avoid civilian deaths as far as it is possible to do so, *and* to minimize the possibility of ever having to use nuclear weapons. This implies a rejection of *both* of the strategies that have been urged by various analysts, that of "countervalue" and "counterforce," for neither of them deals with both of these concerns. Counterforce measures per se, which would have the effect of limiting civilian casualties, require such exacting weapons systems (high accuracy, tight control, relatively high explosive yields, and large numbers of warheads) that they tend to destabilize the nuclear balance (by threatening an opponent's confidence in the security of his retaliatory force) and thereby increase the chance of the use of nuclear weapons in a crisis or war. Countervalue measures seek to reduce the chance of nuclear war by maximizing the probability and horrors of retribution against civilians. Each strategy sees a trade off between policies which seek to

---

62. See Earl C. Ravenal, *Strategic Disengagement and World Peace* (San Francisco: CATO Institute, 1979), pp. 34–39, Nye, op. cit., p. 122, and idem., *Nuclear Ethics* (New York: The Free Press, 1986), pp. 108–115.

reduce civilian casualties in the event of war and those which seek to reduce to a minimum the possibility of war ever occurring. Both principles are compelling ones and the logic of nuclear winter dictates that both be addressed.

The adoption of what Earl Ravenal calls a "countercombatant" doctrine, that is, targeting only a potential opponent's non-nuclear military forces, would seem to represent a first step out of this dilemma.[63] If the Soviet-American strategic balance could be restructured in such a way that neither side could have any incentive—especially in a crisis—to attack the other's retaliatory forces, the twin concerns of (a) reducing damage should war come and (b) minimizing the possibility that war would break out, would appear to be met. In that case, only the traditional sinews of military power would be targeted (armies, tactical command centers, supply lines, etc.). Each side could remain confident that the ultimate guarantor of strategic stability—its nuclear retaliatory capability—would remain secure. As a matter of principle, nuclear retaliatory forces would not be targeted. In practice, the superpowers would strive to reshape their strategic relationship so that it would make no military sense to do so. While strategic nuclear forces would have to be highly accurate and tightly commanded and controlled in order to implement such a strategy, the stability of the nuclear balance would not be upset *if* these forces were relatively invulnerable. This could be secured in a variety of ways, ranging from "de-MIRVing" strategic forces (i.e., reducing the ratio of missile warheads to missiles), the measured introduction of strategic defensive systems to protect strategic bases, to the adoption and implementation of a no-first-use doctrine. The first two measures would reduce the incentive to attack the other side's missiles, since their invulnerability assures a retaliatory attack whose scale and character will be determined by one's opponent (who would then have lost any doubts about one's willingness to use nuclear weapons). The latter would impose a measure of self-restraint in that nuclear weapons would only be used in the event of nuclear attack on one's own territory. Furthermore, even if one's cities were attacked, the opponent's cities would be spared in the second strike. This would have both a moral and an expedient justification: sparing innocent lives is a

---

63. In addition to Ravenal, op. cit., see Jeffrey Richelson, "The Dilemmas of Counterpower Targeting," in Ball and Richelson (eds.), *Strategic Nuclear Targeting*, op. cit., pp. 159–170.

positive ethical imperative in itself; not to spare them would divert nuclear weapons from more significant military targets and, what is more, would risk setting off nuclear winter.

Acceptance of the nuclear winter hypothesis would add one more stringent condition to the eventual use of nuclear weapons. As J.J. Gertler puts it: "If nuclear winter can happen (or if we have reason to believe that it can), the list of possible responses available to National Command Authorities (NCA) in the event of a nuclear strike should include an estimate of the boomerang effect of each use of nuclear weapons. NCA must know the likely effects on the United States of every given detonation before they issue orders."[64] It should be quite apparent that such a requirement practically excludes the use of nuclear weapons at all.

The nuclear winter theory, then, while underscoring the importance of nuclear arms control and reductions, points to the effective dissociation of nuclear weapons from military and foreign policy. Interestingly, George Kennan, father of the "containment" policy, elaborated the logic of such a position in a memorandum prepared for the State Department's policy planning staff in early 1950. In this memorandum, which Kennan considers "to have been in its implications one of the most important, if not the most important, of all the documents" he ever wrote in government, he addressed the relation of nuclear weapons to U.S. foreign and military policy. Kennan argued that

> there was no victory and no security to be won for our people by the sort of destruction these weapons were capable of working.... The victories that mattered would never be real victories unless they involved changes ... in the minds of men; and such changes could never be brought about by destruction, and particularly the destruction of innocent life, on so vast and indiscriminate a scale.[65]

Furthermore, Kennan went on, the mere cultivation of nuclear weapons, in light of their suicidal nature, "would sooner or later present serious problems of public understanding . . . and would raise questions as between ourselves and our allies that would be disruptive in their effect on the workings of existing alliances."[66] Kennan's conception of the place of nuclear weapons in U.S. policy, then, was a most

---

64. Gertler, op. cit., p. 13.
65. George F. Kennan, *Memoirs 1925–1950* (New York: Pantheon Books, 1967), pp. 472, 474.
66. Ibid., p. 474.

restrictive one, and this at the same time that he had helped elaborate a most active foreign policy of containment of the Soviet Union. Nuclear weapons, in Kennan's view, were

> an undesirable necessity, the very existence of which we regretted and deplored—a form of weapon we were obliged to hold because we had no assurance against its development and use by others against us, but the use of which we had no intention of initiating in any military encounter. In this case, we would of course not base plans for defense upon the presumption of its use.[67]

As long as the United States maintained nuclear "superiority" over the Soviet Union, Kennan's logic could be contested by the argument that the possibility of a disarming strike against Soviet nuclear assets enabled the U.S. to secure substantial military and political benefits from its nuclear posture. The nuclear winter theory, however, strongly suggests that even such a strike—which effectively disarmed the opponent—could trigger catastrophic consequences for oneself, thereby rendering inexpedient a strategy whose moral foundations have always been contestable. In that case, Kennan's call for severing the link between nuclear weapons and foreign and defense policy acquires compelling significance.

■ Intra-alliance Relations: NATO and the Warsaw Pact

The United States underwrites the security of its European allies through a nuclear guarantee. This guarantee is fully integrated into NATO strategy, which envisages the possible first-use of nuclear weapons in the face of a purely conventional attack. While nuclear weapons deployed in and around Europe constitute the primary means of implementing this guarantee, it is not excluded that weapons based in the United States itself would be used to turn the tide of battle. Such an arrangement is doubly satisfying to America's allies: anxious to secure a nuclear guarantee from the U.S. which they believe enhances deterrence, the European NATO members do not wish to see that promise implemented should war come. The deployment since late 1983 of U.S. missiles on West European soil that are capable of hitting the Soviet Union is a perfect reflection of this

---

67. Ibid., p. 472.

tension in the attitudes of the European NATO countries. By binding American and West European nuclear fates more closely together, the Pershing II and cruise missiles at the same time are intended to have a "coupling effect" and underscore to Moscow that it cannot separate West European from U.S. security, thereby enhancing deterrence. It is the supposed credibility of the threat that these weapons will in the last resort be used which, in the eyes of the West Europeans, imposes restraint on both the U.S. and USSR.

This strategy of "flexible response" has been in force for nearly two decades now and is the result of a delicate network of compromises and legal fictions between the United States and its West European partners. The most glaring of these, as Henry Kissinger so indelicately pointed out before a stunned European audience in 1979, is that the United States would actually use its nuclear arsenal in defense of its European allies, thereby triggering national suicide.[68] So long as the concept of military victory could be preserved—that is, so long as planners could envision scenarios in which the use of nuclear weapons could advance national political interests—this fiction could be preserved. Whether such scenarios were at all plausible is beside the point. What matters is that it was at least possible to imagine a given disposition of military forces which could yield victory in the event of war.

The theory of nuclear winter exposes such expectations for the illusions many have long thought them, for other reasons, to be. The heavy forestation and urban density in central Europe is such that exchanges of "theater" nuclear weapons, in addition to devastating the region, might themselves create a nuclear winter effect if urban conurbations could not be avoided and if the war escalated, as would seem likely.[69] The distinction between "tactical" and "strategic" nuclear weapons would thereby appear to disappear, since any "tactical" weapon can have "strategic," or global consequences. The possibility that the territory of the United States (or of the Soviet Union for that matter) could escape the consequences of war in Europe would seem to be decisively refuted.

It is important at this point to distinguish the impact of nuclear

---

68. Henry Kissinger, "The Future of NATO," in Kenneth A. Meyers (ed.), *NATO: The Next Thirty Years* (London: Croom Helm, 1980), pp. 7–9.
69. According to Carl Sagan, reported to J.J. Gertler in idem, op. cit., footnote 1, p. 9.

winter on the central Europeans from its impact on the superpowers, and especially on the United States. It is doubtful whether the inhabitants of central Europe, above all the Germans (East and West), will be able to see any meaningful difference between the consequences of nuclear winter for them and the likely results of the short-term effects alone of a nuclear war fought in Europe.[70] But they will be able to grasp the leap in risk which the United States now assumes by continuing to underwrite a nuclear guarantee for NATO Europe. If they accept the theory of nuclear winter, they will have very strong reasons for refusing to accept the credibility of the American nuclear umbrella. If the theater use of nuclear weapons in Europe is sufficient to cause grave damage to the United States, how likely is it that the United States would order a nuclear defense of Europe? Not very. It is very likely, therefore, that doubts about the U.S. commitment to defend Western Europe, which currently depends on a nuclear foundation, will increase as the theory of nuclear winter gains broad public acceptance in Western Europe.

Indeed, in the absence of a thoroughgoing revision of NATO doctrine and capabilities toward a capable non-nuclear deterrent, NATO risks turning itself into a strategic nullity, long the aim of Soviet policy in Western Europe. By continuing its present course NATO will be implicitly choosing to base its security on untenable ground. The West European members will be more skeptical than ever as to the validity of the U.S. security guarantee.[71] The U.S. will in effect have deterred itself by clinging to a strategy whose execution, even if successful in the traditional military sense, would inflict grave, if not mortal damage upon the United States. The Soviet Union, whose strategy does not depend upon nuclear weapons for its effectiveness (though it is well prepared to use them) and which has formally declared a no-first-use policy, can be expected to exploit these tensions between the U.S. and its NATO partners to the hilt. Since nuclear winter would have worldwide consequences, it is very likely that the USSR will find willing accomplices among the non-aligned countries

---

70. See William Arkin et al., "The Consequences of a 'Limited' Nuclear War in East and West Germany," *Ambio*, op. cit., pp. 163–173.
71. A study conducted under the auspices of the U.S. Air Force's Center for Aerospace Doctrine, Research, and Education reached similar conclusions. See *Nuclear Winter and National Security: Implications for Future Policy* (Maxwell Air Force Base, Alabama: Air University Press, July 1986), pp. 70, 21–22.

in its campaign to delegitimize NATO's nuclear policies.* Furthermore, such NATO members as Portugal, Norway, Greece and Turkey, who would probably escape the brunt of attack in the event of war, face a major and qualitatively new threat with the advent of nuclear winter. These countries can be expected to take a greater interest in NATO military and nuclear policies and complicate decision-making, especially with respect to the deployment of nuclear weapons and contingencies for their use.

Even if NATO were to shift its current strategy to a purely conventional one, the existence of independent nuclear deterrents in the British and French nuclear forces would exert a decoupling influence of its own. Carl Sagan estimates that the French *force de frappe*, targeted exclusively on Soviet cities, "may itself be enough to trigger a global Nuclear Winter."[72] "If," as Rand analyst J.J. Gertler notes, "Britain can by itself or in consort with . . . France cause a nuclear winter, the Europeans render the U.S. nuclear deterrent redundant, as American nuclear weapons can threaten no additional harm. Public realization of this fact," Gertler concludes, "could lead to or reinforce calls on both sides of the Atlantic for a decoupling of the U.S. strategic arsenal from European defense (making NATO a conventional-only treaty) and so would drive another wedge into the gap between the allies."[73]

In sum, widespread recognition of the validity of the nuclear winter theory within the NATO countries would tend to further undermine the U.S. promise to use its nuclear weapons, if necessary, to defend Western Europe. As long as NATO refuses to reexamine the nuclear premises behind its current strategy, inexorable decoupling tendencies will make themselves felt in trans-Atlantic alliance relations. Of course, such a reexamination itself could have as divisive effect within the alliance, as divergences of interest and interpretation would have to be explicitly addressed in any reformulation of policy.

---

*The qualitatively new threat that third countries, mainly in the Third World, face because of the nuclear winter phenomenon underlines the condition attached to their adherence to the non-proliferation treaty, i.e., that the nuclear powers would achieve significant nuclear disarmament agreements. The issue can be expected to attract major attention at the 1990 review of the Nuclear Non-Proliferation Treaty, the last before the Treaty comes up for renewal in 1995.

---

72. Letter to *Foreign Affairs*, Spring 1984, p. 1001.
73. Gertler, op. cit., p. 7.

Acceptance of the nuclear winter theory and its military implications in the USSR would have an effect on the countries of the Warsaw Pact as dramatic as that on NATO, though in a very different way. For countries like East Germany, Czechoslovakia and Poland, which would be directly in the line of fire in the event of a nuclear war in Europe, there would probably be little distinction drawn between the immediate and long-term effects of such a war. Consequently, acceptance of the nuclear winter theory would have little if any impact on those countries' policies or position within the Warsaw Pact. The countries of the southern tier of the Warsaw Pact—Hungary, Romania and Bulgaria—would have greater incentive to exert influence on Soviet military policy, since they face a new kind of threat. Unlike their NATO counterparts, however, they have fewer means for making such concerns felt.

For the USSR, though, acceptance of the military implications of the nuclear winter theory would mean a serious reevaluation of its attitude to Eastern Europe. The radical denuclearization that nuclear winter implies would reattach a territorial value to Eastern Europe for the USSR that had been significantly diminished by the onset of the nuclear era. Eastern Europe would reassume the status of traditional military buffer that had been reduced in value with the invention of the nuclear-charged ballistic missile. Consequently, the USSR could be expected to pay closer and more systematic attention to developments within Eastern Europe, as these would be seen to have even more immediate security implications for the USSR than has been the case in recent decades. On the military level, the USSR would be likely to press the East Europeans to increase their military expenditures and to make a more effective contribution to the "common" defense in general. Soviet pressure for tight military, and economic, integration within the Warsaw Pact would probably intensify. On the political level, parties and governments in Eastern Europe would find it increasingly difficult to extend their room for independent maneuver, as the USSR attempted to reassert tighter control over this reborn territorial buffer in the heart of Europe.

A note of qualification: These are not predictions. This analysis of the probable effect of the nuclear winter theory on alliance relations in East and West depends on several conditions obtaining: first, that the nuclear winter theory is in fact accepted; second, that NATO does not consciously recast its strategy to make its security independent of nuclear forces; and finally, that the politico-military situation in Europe is such that the USSR feels it cannot dispense with an extensive territorial buffer in Europe. If any one of these conditions does not prevail, the likely consequences would almost certainly be quite different.

4
The Necessity for Political Leadership

The apparent receptivity of the Soviet leadership to the theory of nuclear winter, and thus to the idea that even the "successful" use of nuclear weapons might bring irreparable harm to the Soviet Union, provides the essential precondition for a multilateral discussion on the need and instrumentalities for bringing about a restructuring of the strategic nuclear nuclear balance worldwide. As a first step toward initiating such a discussion, the USSR and the U.S. might consider an exchange of information on the effects of nuclear winter. Both governments have been reticent on this score. The United States, as already indicated, has refused to permit Soviet scientists to use American "supercomputers" to develop more accurate modeling techniques for measuring the climatic consequences of nuclear war. Soviet scientists have been most reluctant to divulge such critical information as "the particle size distribution function" of debris from the Soviet atmospheric nuclear tests before the 1963 Limited Test-Ban Treaty; information on particle sizes and absorption coefficients from large fires in the Soviet Union; and the range of nuclear war scenarios they consider likely.[74]

Both countries stand to profit from sharing the information they are currently denying the other. What if the U.S. government were to permit Soviet scientists, under appropriately controlled circumstances, to use U.S. supercomputers to test the nuclear winter theory in exchange for information that only the Soviet Union can supply, such as that indicated above? This could take place in the context of a joint meeting of political and military leaders of both countries, perhaps as a working group akin to the Soviet-American discussions

---

74. *Bulletin of the Atomic Scientists*, April 1984, pp. 1–15 S.

on regional issues, to discuss the facts and implications of "nuclear winter." The benefits would be considerable: each government would gain access to information currently not available to it; each would be more certain that the other appreciates the likely climatic consequences of nuclear war; and, it would provide a highly symbolic token of each government's recognition of the need to begin the radical restructuring of their strategic nuclear forces that acceptance of the nuclear winter hypothesis requires. Precedents for such actions in U.S.–Soviet relations exist. In December 1962 President Kennedy unilaterally conveyed to the Soviet leadership certain technical command and control procedures for nuclear forces ("permissive-action links") designed to minimize the possibility of the unauthorized launching of nuclear weapons. This dramatic, though little known action, underscored the common interest that both the U.S. and USSR have in the stability of the nuclear balance. President Kennedy perceived that the U.S. had no interest in preserving an American monopoly on information that, if shared with the Soviet Union, would enhance strategic stability. Traditional notions of military secrecy, he saw, do not hold in such conditions. The same applies to the data on "nuclear winter." It does the U.S. no good, and possibly much harm, to deny the USSR the methodological foundation needed to test and confirm the soundness of the nuclear winter hypothesis.

To sum up, the nuclear winter theory, in the way that it challenges the very concept of nuclear victory, effectively severs the connection between the operational use of nuclear weapons and foreign and defense policy. The theory also demands a reorientation of the global nuclear balance toward minimum deterrent forces whose total explosive force would be less than that deemed necessary to trigger nuclear winter. It requires a targeting doctrine that eschews both "counterforce" and "countervalue" strategies, one in which the non-nuclear armed forces of the opposing side become the only legitimate target of military forces, nuclear or otherwise. In order to ensure that the transition to such a strategy does not prove destabilizing, it will be necessary to redesign strategic forces in such a way that a decapitating first strike becomes inconceivable. This would involve a combination of measures, including a transition to single-warhead missiles. These missiles would have to be highly accurate, of relatively low explosive force, under tight centralized command and control, and as invulnerable as possible. This would help insure that they would be capable of discriminating between civilian and military targets, that they would provide no incentive for preemption by an opponent, and that, should events get out of control, such a force could not pose the threat of unleashing nuclear winter. (The requirements for using such weapons by themselves would be so strict as to practically exclude the incorporation of nuclear weapons into one's general military-political strategy.) Once a framework for reductions in offensive arms had been worked out among the nuclear powers, consideration could be given to the gradual and limited introduction of anti-missile systems. This would provide insurance against cheating and thus an incentive to observe the new strategic order. The new arms control regime would be monitored by a combination of national-technical means and an international inspectorate. Over time, experience with such an internationalized arms control regime could furnish the basis for moving towards actual nuclear disarmament and true international control of nuclear weapons.

Of course, resistance to such a prescription will in all probability prove very strong. Nuclear winter challenges too many of the assumptions of the nuclear age for its implications to be easily digested. The strongest temptation will be to do nothing. After all, the argument might go, we have lived with the objective threat of nuclear winter for over three decades. The world has not collapsed. For all the imperfections of the status quo, real interests are served by it. To depart from it would open up uncertainties whose consequences cannot be foretold.

This argument might hold save for the fact that the key to understanding the strategic implications of nuclear winter are primarily subjective. Once the validity of the theory has been admitted, the conditions which have supported the postwar strategic order up to now are irreparably altered. It is not a question of weighing a certain status quo against an uncertain future. The future, after all, will always be uncertain. The real issue involves a status quo whose foundation is profoundly challenged by the nuclear winter theory and the damages that will ensue if the implications of the theory are not taken into account. As sketched earlier in the paper, these involve the further erosion of the U.S. nuclear guarantee to Western Europe; greater Soviet pressure for strict political, economic, and military conformity in Eastern Europe (due to the increased value of Eastern Europe as a territorial buffer); and the willful continuation of a defense posture and strategy whose execution would bring about the very catastrophe it is designed to prevent. Doing nothing is not an option.

Much more likely would be the attempt by the military in the

Soviet Union and the United States to incorporate the implications of nuclear winter into their force planning and targeting and in this way preserve the credibility of their operational plans for the use of nuclear weapons. One of the first U.S. military officers to take note of the theory was Vice Admiral J. A. Lyons, deputy of naval operations. In an internal memo dated November 7, 1983, Lyons noted that, "In the long term, the [results] deserve serious study to see what, if any, changes in U.S. targeting policy are required," and proposed that the Navy conduct a careful nuclear targeting study.[75]

A series of technical fixes are conceivable whereby the military would attempt to minimize the possibility of nuclear winter while preserving maximum latitude for the execution of nuclear options. J.J. Gertler has described a number of such options, including:

- use of smaller, low-yield weapons on highly accurate delivery systems to attack an opponent's command and control infrastructure rather than command personnel or large facilities like airfields and silo complexes, thereby crippling a foe's retaliatory capacity with minimal nuclear winter effects;
- the use of enhanced-radiation weapons (neutron bombs) to eliminate command personnel;
- greater reliance on chemical weapons;
- greater use of earth-penetrating nuclear munitions (as the blast and heat effects will be partially absorbed by the surrounding dirt): this might offer the possibility of striking targets near a city without igniting the city itself, perhaps giving substance to the idea of a truly surgical strike;
- the use of high-altitude detonations to generate a large electromagnetic pulse that would disrupt the communications on an opponent's territory and thereby paralyze his responses;
- the development of alternate intelligence-gathering measures, since optical satellites would be effectively blinded as soot fills the earth's atmosphere—otherwise, it would not be possible to detect long-term delayed launches from reloadable silos;
- evaluation of the erosion and friction effects of an upper-altitude soot layer on outbound missiles, which could cause damage and/or gross inaccuracy.

This leads Gertler to postulate an ideal nuclear first-strike scenario for a nation that seeks to preempt its opponent's retaliatory capability

---

75. *Science*, July 6, 1984, p. 31.

with minimal nuclear winter effects: "generation of a large EMP [electromagnetic pulse] through high-altitude detonations followed by low-yield counterforce strikes with ERW [neutron bombs] and penetrators."[76]

Gertler's approach, while technically attractive to military planners seeking to preserve their options in an environment that is progressively more hostile to the use of nuclear weapons, suffers from the same deficiencies as all such "limited nuclear options"—the presumption that nuclear use can be carefully controlled, without serious damage to oneself, and the impulse toward preemption, the only scenario in which nuclear use makes any military sense at all. The combination of these factors heightens the tendencies toward strategic instability present in the nuclear balance of power, as each side comes to fear losing its options should it wait and strike second. Furthermore, the ever present "risk of losing control," in Albert Wohlstetter's words,[77] brings us back to the problem which the limited war approach seeks to avoid—large-scale nuclear war, and so nuclear winter and its related climatological, ecological, social and biological consequences.

Political leadership of the most exacting sort will be required to avoid the attempt to reconcile the prospect of nuclear winter with the prosecution of nuclear war. Our politicians will have to explain to the American people the necessity for the kind of radical strategic nuclear disengagement demanded by nuclear winter, and they will have to be capable of enforcing this understanding on the military and its operational planning. Soviet politicians will have to do likewise. They will have to negotiate this understanding with each other, with the other nuclear powers and with the rest of the world, and make it stick.

There are a number of steps of a collaborative and unilateral character that the Soviet Union and the United States could take to propel this process of nuclear disengagement forward. Each would respond to a particular concern raised by the nuclear winter theory.

First, the U.S. and USSR should agree, in the context of the Geneva strategic arms negotiations, on a set of principles for the *long-term* reduction and restructuring of their offensive nuclear forces. The 50 percent reductions that are now the subject of negotiation would be understood to constitute a first step toward a radical reduction of

---

76. Gertler, *op. cit.*, pp. 10–13.
77. Wohlstetter, *op. cit.*, p. 990.

offensive weapons that would objectively preclude the possibility of nuclear winter. This need not occupy the negotiators in the immediate future; the task of negotiating a 50 percent reduction is formidable enough. Yet it would be a tremendous step forward if both sides could agree on a set of operational principles envisioning the eventual reduction of nuclear forces below the nuclear winter threshold.

Second, both countries should establish a permanent joint working group that would examine ways of enhancing strategic stability during the transition to a substantially denuclearized world. While at first this would necessarily be a Soviet-American body, it would eventually have to be expanded to include the other nuclear powers, as well as representatives from non-nuclear states. Since in the long term, any disarmament regime responding to the nuclear winter threat would have to be internationalized (considering the very limited forces capable of triggering the nuclear winter effect, as well as the global consequences of the phenomenon), the working group on strategic stability should be put under United Nations auspices, possibly in connection with the Committee on Disarmament in Geneva.

Third, both the U.S. and USSR, as well as the other European countries, need to intensify their exploration of more collaborative approaches to security, especially in Europe. A positive value in itself, this enterprise assumes all the more importance if the radically denuclearized world implied by the nuclear winter theory is not to make the world safe for a frightfully destructive conventional war. Both NATO and the Warsaw Pact countries need to be reassured that the changed strategic environment herein envisioned will not detract from their security. Otherwise, the political-military consequences of denuclearization could be quite destabilizing. The CSCE process (Conference on Security and Cooperation in Europe) provides a natural vehicle for the elaboration of more collaborative security measures.

Fourth, as a unilateral measure, the U.S. should proceed discussing with its NATO partners ways of initiating a process of the eventual denuclearization of NATO's strategy. While the nuclear winter theory appears to undermine extended *nuclear* deterrence as a policy, the credibility of the U.S. commitment to defend Western Europe will not be undermined if NATO gradually transfers the foundation of that commitment from an explicitly nuclear to a conventional one. Again, this would have to be done in a measured fashion, so that the transitional instabilities of moving from one deterrent system to another are not greater than the instabilities in the existing system. Such a transition would not remove the possibility of U.S. nuclear retaliation as a last resort. It would, however, preserve the force of the U.S. commitment, which otherwise would be undercut by the challenge offered by the nuclear winter theory to all nuclear threats (and promises).

Finally, both the U.S. and USSR should immediately reorient their strategic targeting plans so that under no circumstances would cities, or other highly combustible targets (e.g., oil refineries), be attacked in the event of war. Each power can undertake this step independently of the other and in advance of actual arms reduction and force transformations. Regardless of stated intentions, in a crisis governments will tend to behave within the limits imposed by preexisting plans. If the plans can be altered to remove the single most dangerous option of all—targeting cities—an enormous preliminary step toward nuclear sanity would have been taken.

But what, it may sensibly be asked, if the nuclear winter theory turns out to be wrong, as scientific theories are wont to do? Would the kinds of measures recommended above thereby lose their validity? Does so much hinge on the nuclear winter theory itself? In the first place, there has been a truly impressive breadth of scientific consensus behind the principle of a nuclear winter effect. The precise magnitude of the effect and a variety of technical processes are still, legitimately, subject to research and discussion. At this point, though, it appears highly improbable that the concept as such is off the mark. Secondly, I have argued that the theory is most important for the way it encapsulates the basic truth of the nuclear age—that nuclear "weapons" are not, and cannot be, under foreseeable circumstances, instruments of warfare, and thus of policy. If even the militarily "successful" use of nuclear weapons threatens oneself, one's allies, and much of the rest of the world with grave, and potentially catastrophic damage, it simply highlights on a conceptual level what the fact of "mutual assured destruction" has done in reality, since with assured retaliatory capabilities no successful use of the nuclear arm is plausible. Refutation of the theory of nuclear winter would not change this basic situation. Henning Wegener, the West German Ambassador to the U.N. Committee on Disarmament in Geneva, put the matter succinctly when he noted that:

The mere theoretical possibility of nuclear winter sharpens the dilemma of the nuclear age, heightens the paradox of the nuclear weapon which, simultaneously, functions as the potential destroyer of life and the ultimate preserver of world peace. It heightens the paradox, but does not eliminate it. By increasing the margins of uncertainty about the effects of any major use of the nuclear instrument, i.e., by increasing the risks inherent in a future war, the current debate strengthens the case for the elimination of war—of all wars—as a political instrument.[78]

Many of the policy choices urged in this paper, then, follow from this broader logic of the nuclear age: radical reductions respond to the dictate to reduce damage in the event that nuclear war, ever a present possibility, should indeed come about; concern about stability is justified for its own sake, and increases with significant reductions in force levels; increased attention to conventional issues makes sense as a prudent safeguard in the face of nuclear stalemate; while a no-cities targeting doctrine meets long-standing moral concern without in the process either undermining deterrence or provoking preemptive instabilities. Given the general plausibility of the theory, however, the measures suggested above seem prudent and cost-effective hedges against an eventuality entailing truly dire consequences.

A final point to consider is that it took nearly four decades for the nuclear winter idea to come to light. Even if the concept as such should prove false, as seems unlikely, what other inherently unforeseeable consequences of nuclear war, magnified by the synergistic confluence of physical, atmospheric, ecological, agricultural, and social factors, remain to be discovered, in theory or, God forbid, in practice?[79] The truth is that, given this recognition, the kinds of implications suggested by the theory of nuclear winter applied as much at the dawn of the atomic age as they do today.

---

78. Henning Wegener, "The Nuclear-Winter Hypothesis: Some Personal Reflections," *Disarmament*, Autumn 1984, p. 74.
79. The single, "unforeseeable" accident at the Chernobyl nuclear power plant in the Ukraine in April 1986 cast a radioactive swath from the Scandinavian Arctic through the Middle East (with remnants traceable as far away as Oregon), with the effect, *inter alia*, of destroying local fish industries in Italy and the reindeer economy of the Laplanders in Sweden and Finland. See *The New York Times*, May 27, 1986, p. A2, May 29, 1986, p. A23 and the report of the *London Observer* as reprinted in *Newsday*, July 28, 1986, p. 13. The vulnerability of nuclear power stations to nuclear attack, and the incalculable consequences of the most limited strike affecting them, has barely been examined. See Bennett Ramberg, "Targeting Nuclear Energy," in Ball and Richelson (eds.), *Strategic Nuclear Targeting*, op. cit. pp. 250–266.

The task outlined here is a demanding one, especially for the United States, which will have to reshape much of its military policy and the foundation for its foreign policy, long far too dependent on the threat of using nuclear weapons. Nevertheless, the rewards will be great, for it was only with the advent of the nuclear weapon that the United States itself became militarily vulnerable. Nuclear disengagement would substantially relieve the United States of this sole threat to its existence. It would also help to demilitarize much of our thinking about American foreign policy and highlight those areas in which the United States has a true comparative advantage over the Soviet Union: in the economy; in a vibrant, cosmopolitan culture; and in a free society which is both a positive value in itself and the best encouragement to the kind of scientific creativity that will determine the shape of the world in the centuries ahead.

Perhaps the most compelling reasons to initiate consideration of the types of measures suggested in this paper, however, are those of moral character. George Kennan, the father of containment, put the issue squarely in 1980 in what were probably the most impassioned lines of his life. Directing his words to the Soviet and American leadership, Kennan declared:

> You are mortal men. You are capable of error. You have no right to hold in your hands—there is no one wise enough and strong enough to hold in his hands—destructive powers sufficient to put an end to civilized life on a great portion of our planet.
>
> No one should wish to have in his hands such power.[80]

The specific features of the nuclear winter phenomenon, which raises a qualitatively new threat to countries outside the direct line of fire between the leading nuclear powers, highlight the question posed by U.N. Secretary-General Javier Perez de Cuellar in a December 1984 speech: "by what right do they decide the fate of all humanity?"[81] The question has yet to receive a serious answer.

In this light, the threat represented by the prospect of nuclear winter is actually an unprecedented opportunity for man to reassert control over his destiny. By tapping the elemental sources of nature, man has managed to array the wrath of nature against him. And yet the

---

80. Cited in Barton Gellman, *Contending with Kennan. Toward a Philosophy of American Power* (New York: Praeger, 1984), p. 77.
81. Javier Perez de Cuellar, "Secretary General's Statement to General Assembly on Disarmament Issues" (New York: United Nations, SG/SM3635, December 12, 1984).

threat is not natural, but rather artificially induced. Human intervention created this threat. Human intervention can end it. The conditions exist. Is man capable of seizing this opportunity and thereby proving himself worthy of the human vocation?

Select Bibliography on Nuclear Winter and Long-Term Consequences of Nuclear War

Adams, Ruth and Cullen, Susan, editors. *The Final Epidemic: Physicians and Scientists on Nuclear War.* Chicago: Educational Foundation for Nuclear Science, 1981.

Arkin, William et al. "The Consequences of a 'Limited' Nuclear War in East and West Germany," *Ambio*, vol. 11, no. 2–3 (1982), pp. 163–173.

Ball, Desmond and Richelson, Jeffrey, editors. *Strategic Nuclear Targeting.* Ithaca, NY: Cornell University Press, 1986.

Barnaby, Frank and Rotblat, Joseph. "The Effects of Nuclear Weapons," *Ambio*, vol. 11, no. 2–3 (1982), pp. 84–93.

Batten, E.S. *The Effects of Nuclear War on the Weather and Climate.* Santa Monica: The Rand Corporation, Memorandum RM-4989 TB, August 1966.

Bondietti, Ernest A. "Effects on Agriculture," *Ambio*, vol. 11, no. 2–3 (1982), pp. 138–142.

Center for Aerospace Doctrine, Research, and Education (U.S. Air Force). *Nuclear Winter and National Security: Implications for Future Policy.* Maxwell Air Force Base, Alabama: Air University Press, July 1986.

Chazov, Yevgeny I., Il'in, L.A., and Guskova, A.K. *Yadernaya voyna: mediko-biologicheskiye posledstviya. Tochka zreniya sovetskikh uchenykh-medikov* [Nuclear War: Medical-Biological Consequences. The Viewpoint of Soviet Scientists and Doctors]. Moscow: Novosti, 1984.

Crutzen, Paul J. and Birks, John W. "The Atmosphere After a Nuclear War: Twilight at Noon," *Ambio*, vol. 11, no. 2–3 (1982), pp. 114–125.

Department of Defense. "Technical Issues Update," submitted to the Senate Armed Services Committee, May 9, 1986.

Ehrlich, Anne. "Nuclear Winter," *Bulletin of the Atomic Scientists*, April 1984, pp. 3C–14C.

Ehrlich, Paul R. et al., editors. *The Cold and the Dark. The World After Nuclear War.* New York: Norton, 1984.

Ehrlich, Paul R. et al. "Long-Term Biological Consequences of Nuclear War," *Science*, vol. 222, no. 4630 (December 23, 1983), pp. 1293–1300.

Fyodorov, Yury. " 'Yadernaya zima' i yaderni kurs S.Sh.A." ["Nuclear Winter" and U.S. Nuclear Policy], *Mirovaya Ekonomika i Mezhdunarodyne Otnosheniya*, no. 6 (June 1986), pp. 77–82.

Gertler, J.J. *Some Policy Implications of Nuclear Winter.* Washington, D.C.: The Rand Corporation, January 1985.

Ginzburg, Aleksandr S. " 'Yadernaya zima'—Real'naya Ugroza Chelovechestvu" ["Nuclear Winter"—a Real Threat to Mankind], *S.Sh.A.* (Moscow), no. 3 (March 1985), pp. 50–59.

Gleick, James. "Less Drastic Theory Emerges on Freezing After a Nuclear War," *The New York Times*, June 22, 1986, pp. 1, 20.

Goure, Leon. " 'Nuclear Winter' in Soviet Mirrors," *Strategic Review*, Summer 1985, pp. 23–38.

Gray, Colin. "The Nuclear Winter Thesis and U.S. Strategic Policy," *The Washington Quarterly*, Summer 1985, pp. 89–96.

Harwell, Mark A. *Nuclear Winter. The Human and Environmental Consequences of Nuclear War.* New York: Springer-Verlag, 1984.

Hjort, Howard W. "The Impact on Global Food Supplies," *Ambio*, vol. 11, no. 2–3 (1982), pp. 153–157.

Hoeber, Francis P. and Squire, Robert K. "The 'Nuclear Winter' Hypothesis: Some Policy Implications," *Strategic Review*, Summer 1985, pp. 39–46.

Horowitz, Dan and Lieber, Robert J. "Nuclear Winter and the Future of Deterrence," *The Washington Quarterly*, Summer 1985, pp. 59–70.

Kapitsa, Sergei. "Global Consequences of a Nuclear War and the World After," *Disarmament*, Spring 1985, pp. 121–131.

———. "A Soviet View of Nuclear Winter," *Bulletin of the Atomic Scientists*, October 1985, pp. 37–39.

———. "Nauchit'sya Dumat' Po-Novomu" [Learning to Think in New Categories], *Inostrannaya Literatura*, no. 1 (January 1986), pp. 199–206.

Long-Term Worldwide Effects of Multiple Nuclear-Weapons Detonations. Washington, D.C.: National Academy of Sciences, 1975.

National Academy of Sciences. *The Effects on the Atmosphere of a Major Nuclear Exchange.* Washington, D.C.: National Academy Press, 1985.

Nye, Joseph S., Jr. "Nuclear Winter and Policy Choices," *Survival*, March/April 1986, pp. 119–127.

Powers, Thomas. "Nuclear Winter and Nuclear Strategy," *The Atlantic Monthly*, November 1984, pp. 53–64.

Quester, George. "Nuclear Winter: Bad News, No News, or Good News?" in Quester, *The Future of Nuclear Deterrence*. Lexington, MA: Lexington Books, 1986, pp. 121–144.

Raloff, Jane. "Nuclear Winter: Shutting Down the Farm?" *Science News*, September 14, 1985, pp. 171–173.

Rathjens, George W. and Siegel, Ronald H. "Nuclear Winter: Strategic Significance," *Issues in Science and Technology*, Winter 1985, pp. 123–128.

Romero, Philip J. *Nuclear Winter: Implications for U.S. and Soviet Nuclear Strategy.* The Rand Paper Series, no. P-7009-RGI, December 1984.

Sagan, Carl. "Nuclear War and Climatic Catastrophe: Some Policy Implications," *Foreign Affairs*, Winter 1983/84, pp. 257–292. See *Foreign Affairs*, Spring 1984 for commentary, pp. 995–1002.

Scientific Committee on Problems of the Environment (International Council of Scientific Unions). *Environmental Consequences of Nuclear War*. Volume I. Physical and Atmospheric Effects, by A. Barrie Pittock, Thomas P. Ackerman, Paul J. Crutzen, Michael C. MacCracken, Charles S. Schapiro, and Richard P. Turco (Chichester: John Wiley & Sons, 1986); Volume II. Ecological and Agricultural Effects, by Mark A. Harwell and Thomas C. Hutchinson (Chichester: John Wiley & Sons, 1985).

Singer, S. Fred. "Nuclear Winter and Nuclear Freeze," *Disarmament*, Autumn 1984, pp. 63–72.

Sparks, Brad. "Lysenko's Ghost. The Scandal of Nuclear Winter," *National Review*, November 15, 1985, pp. 23–38.

Thompson, Starley L. and Schneider, Stephen H. "Nuclear Winter Reappraised," *Foreign Affairs*, Summer 1986, pp. 981–1005. See commentary on this article in *Foreign Affairs*, Fall 1986, pp. 163–178.

Turco, R.P. et al. "Nuclear Winter: Global Consequences of Multiple Nuclear Explosions," *Science*, Volume 222, no. 4630 (December 23, 1983), pp. 1283–1292.

U.S., Congress, Office of Technology Assessment; *The Effects of Nuclear War*. Washington, D.C.: U.S. Government Printing Office, 1979.

U.S., Congress, Senate, Committee on Armed Services, *Nuclear Winter and its Implications*, 99th Cong., 1st sess., 2–3 October 1985 Washington, D.C.: Government Printing Office, 1986.

Velikhov, Yevgeny, editor. *The Night After*. Moscow: Mir Publishers, 1985. Published in Russian as *Noch' Posle*. Moscow: Nauka, 1985.

Voter Options on Nuclear Arms Policy. New York: The Public Agenda Foundation, 1984.

"Washington Forum on the World-wide Consequences of Nuclear War" of December 8, 1983 (abridged transcript), *Disarmament*, Autumn 1984, pp. 33–62.

Wegener, Henning. "The Nuclear-Winter Hypothesis: Some Personal Reflections," *Disarmament*, Autumn 1984, pp. 73–80.

Weinberger, Caspar W., Secretary of Defense. *The Potential Effects of Nuclear War on the Climate*. A Report to the United States Congress. March 1985. *Congressional Record*, March 6, 1985, pp. S2580–S2585.

Wohlstetter, Albert. "Between an Unfree World and None," *Foreign Affairs*, Summer 1985, pp. 962–994.

Institute For East-West Security Studies
BOARD OF DIRECTORS

CO-CHAIRMEN OF THE BOARD

Academician Ivan T. Berend
President
Hungarian Academy of Sciences, Budapest

Whitney MacMillan
Chairman and Chief Executive Officer
Cargill, Inc., Minnetonka, Minn.

PRESIDENT
John Edwin Mroz
Institute for East-West Security Studies
New York

CHAIRMAN OF THE EXECUTIVE COMMITTEE
Ira D. Wallach
Chairman of the Board
Central National-Gottesman Inc., New York

HONORARY CHAIRMAN OF THE BOARD
Dr. h.c. Berthold Beitz
President
Alfried Krupp von Bohlen und
Halbach-Foundation, Essen

CO-CHAIRMEN OF THE ACADEMIC ADVISORY COMMITTEE

Professor Curt Gasteyger
Director
Programme for Strategic and International Security Studies
Graduate Institute of International Studies, Geneva

Professor Janusz Symonides
Director
Polish Institute of International Affairs, Warsaw

Dr. Antonio Armellini
Special Adviser to the Minister of Transport, Rome

Professor Seweryn Bialer
Director, Research Institute on International Change
Columbia University, New York

The Hon. Lawrence Eagleburger
President
Kissinger Associates, New York

H.E. Ferenc Esztergalyos
Ambassador, Permanent Mission of the Hungarian People's Republic to the United Nations, New York

Michael V. Forrestal, Esq.
Shearman & Sterling, New York

Dr. hab. Ryszard Frelek
Chief, Division for Political Strategy
Academy of Social Sciences, Warsaw

H.E. Robert Garai
Director, Hungarian Institute of International Relations, Budapest

H. E. Mr. Ignac Golob
Undersecretary for Foreign Affairs, Belgrade

David C. Gompert
Vice President, Civil Sales
AT&T, Washington, D.C.

Rita E. Hauser, Esq.
Chairperson of the IEWSS Budget and Audit Committee
Senior Partner
Stroock & Stroock & Lavan, New York

H.E. Dr. Johan Jorgen Holst*
Minister of Defense, Oslo

H. E. Peter Jankowitsch*
Minister for Foreign Affairs, Vienna

*On leave of absence for government service.

Professor Dr. Karl Kaiser
Director
Research Institute of the German Society for Foreign Policy, Bonn

Donald Kendall
Chairman of the Executive Committee
PepsiCo, Inc., New York

H.E. Dr. Keijo Korhonen
Permanent Ambassador
Mission of Finland to the United Nations, New York

Flora Lewis
Foreign Affairs Columnist
The New York Times, Paris

Dr. Manuel Medina Ortega
Vice President, European Parliament
Madrid

Albert J. Moorman, Jr., Esq.
McCutchen, Doyle, Brown & Enersen
San Francisco

Professor Thierry de Montbrial
Director, French Institute of International Relations, Paris

Pauline Neville-Jones
Director, Policy Planning, Foreign & Commonwealth Office, London

Dr. Jan Pudlak
Director, Institute for Foreign Relations, Prague

Professor Dr. Klaus Ritter
Director, Foundation for Science and Policy, Ebenhausen

The Hon. Olin C. Robison
Chairperson of the IEWSS Nominating Committee
President, Middlebury College
Middlebury, Vermont

Daniel Rose
President, Rose Associates, New York

Harold H. Saunders
Visiting Fellow, The Brookings Institution, Washington, D.C.

Professor Dr. Max Schmidt
Director, Institute of International Politics and Economics
Berlin, German Democratic Republic

Dr. Eleanor B. Sheldon
Business Consultant, New York

Mitchell I. Sonkin, Esq.
Secretary of the Institute
Pryor, Cashman, Sherman & Flynn
New York

Helmut Sonnenfeldt
Guest Scholar, The Brookings Institution
Washington, D.C.

Michael I. Sovern
President, Columbia University
New York

H.E. Mr. Emmanuel S. Spyridakis
Ambassador of Greece to Yugoslavia
Belgrade

Dietrich Stobbe
Member of the Bundestag, Bonn

Stephen C. Swid
Treasurer of the Institute
Chairman and Chief Executive Officer
SBK Entertainment World, New York

Peter Tarnoff
President, Council on Foreign Relations
New York

Dr. Seyfi Tashan
President, Turkish Institute of Foreign Policy, Ankara

Thomas J. Tisch
Chairperson of the IEWSS Finance Committee
Managing Partner, FLF Associates, Inc.
New York

Jeremy P. Waletzky, M.D.
Washington, D.C.

H.E. Mr. Guenther van Well
Ambassador of the Federal Republic of Germany to the United States
Washington, D.C.

Occasional Paper Series

1 **Confidence-Building Measures and U.S.-Soviet Relations**
F. Stephen Larrabee & Allen Lynch

2 **No-First-Use: A Window of Opportunity?**
Istvan Farago

3 **The Political Role of Nuclear Weapons: No-First-Use and the Stability of the European Order**
Josef Joffe

4 **Asia and the Pacific: Another Dimension of East-West Relations**
J.D.B. Miller

5 **Political and Military Implications of the "Nuclear Winter" Theory**
Allen Lynch

Institute for East-West Security Studies
360 Lexington Avenue
New York, New York 10017

ISBN 0-8133-0658-2 (Westview)